**ADVANCED READING: GUITAR**

# ADVANCED READING STUDIES FOR GUITAR

Positions Eight Through Twelve and Multi-Position Studies in All Keys

William Leavitt

**Berklee Press**
Director: Dave Kusek
Managing Editor: Debbie Cavalier
Marketing Manager: Ola Frank
Sr. Writer/Editor: Jonathan Feist

ISBN 0-634-01337-8

1140 Boylston Street
Boston, MA 02215-3693 USA
(617) 747-2146

Visit Berklee Press Online at
**www.berkleepress.com**

7777 W. Bluemound Rd. P.O. Box 13819
Milwaukee, Wisconsin 53213

Visit Hal Leonard Online at
**www.halleonard.com**

Copyright © 1981 Berklee Press
All Rights Reserved

No part of this publication may be reproduced in any form or by any means without the prior written permission of the Publisher.

# 8th POSITION

**MAJOR SCALES**

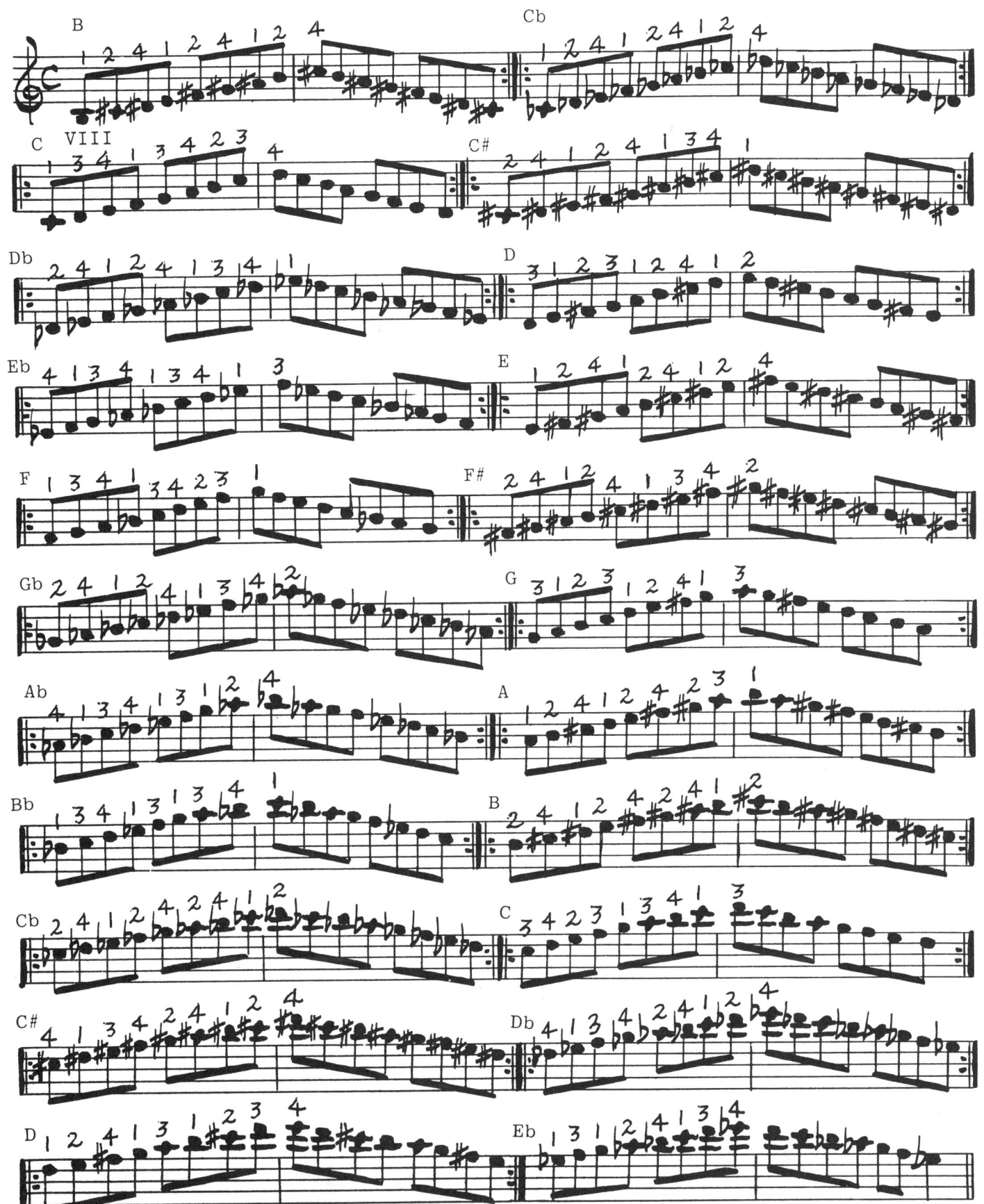

## HARMONIC MINOR SCALES

# SYMMETRIC SCALES

CHROMATIC

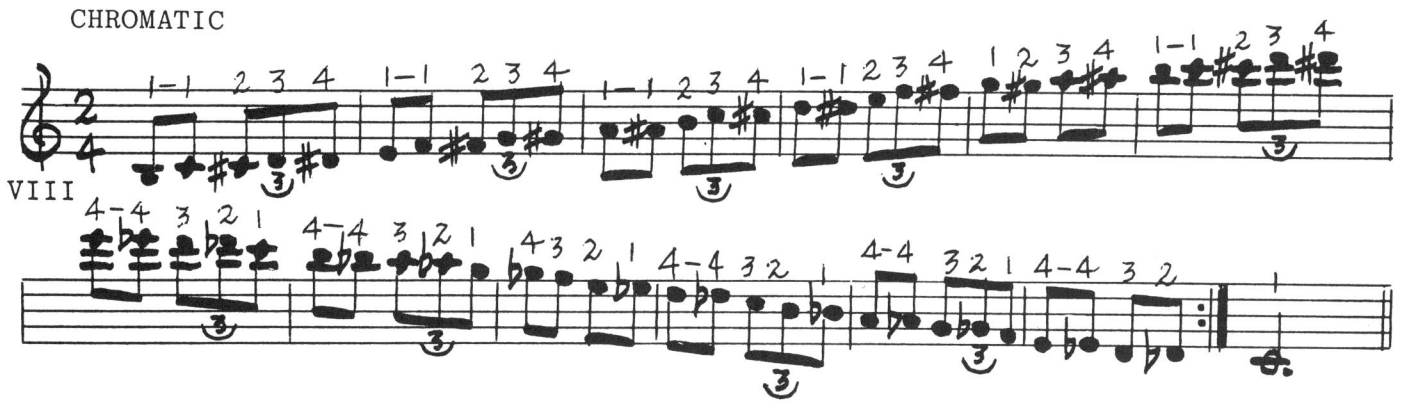

WHOLE TONE

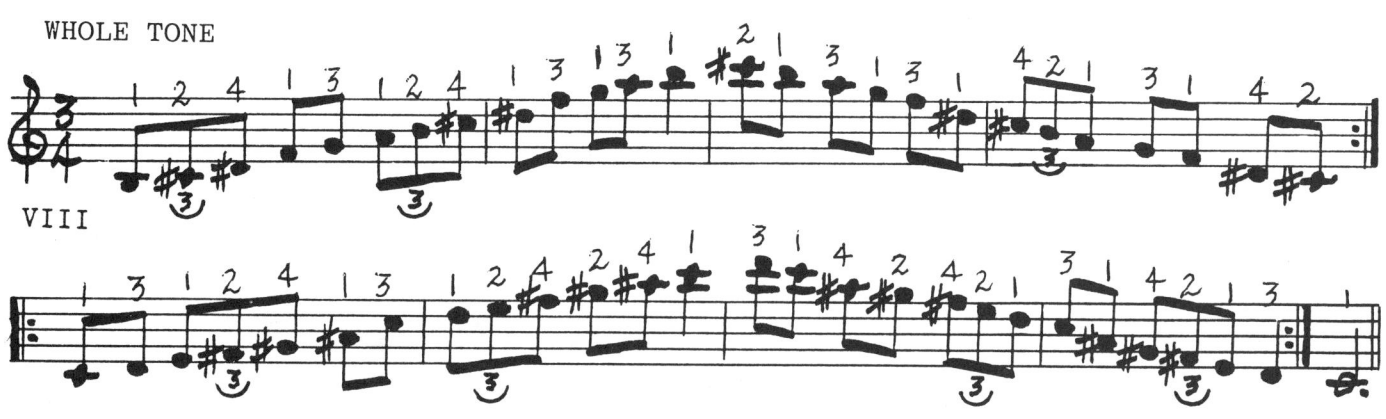

DIMINISHED

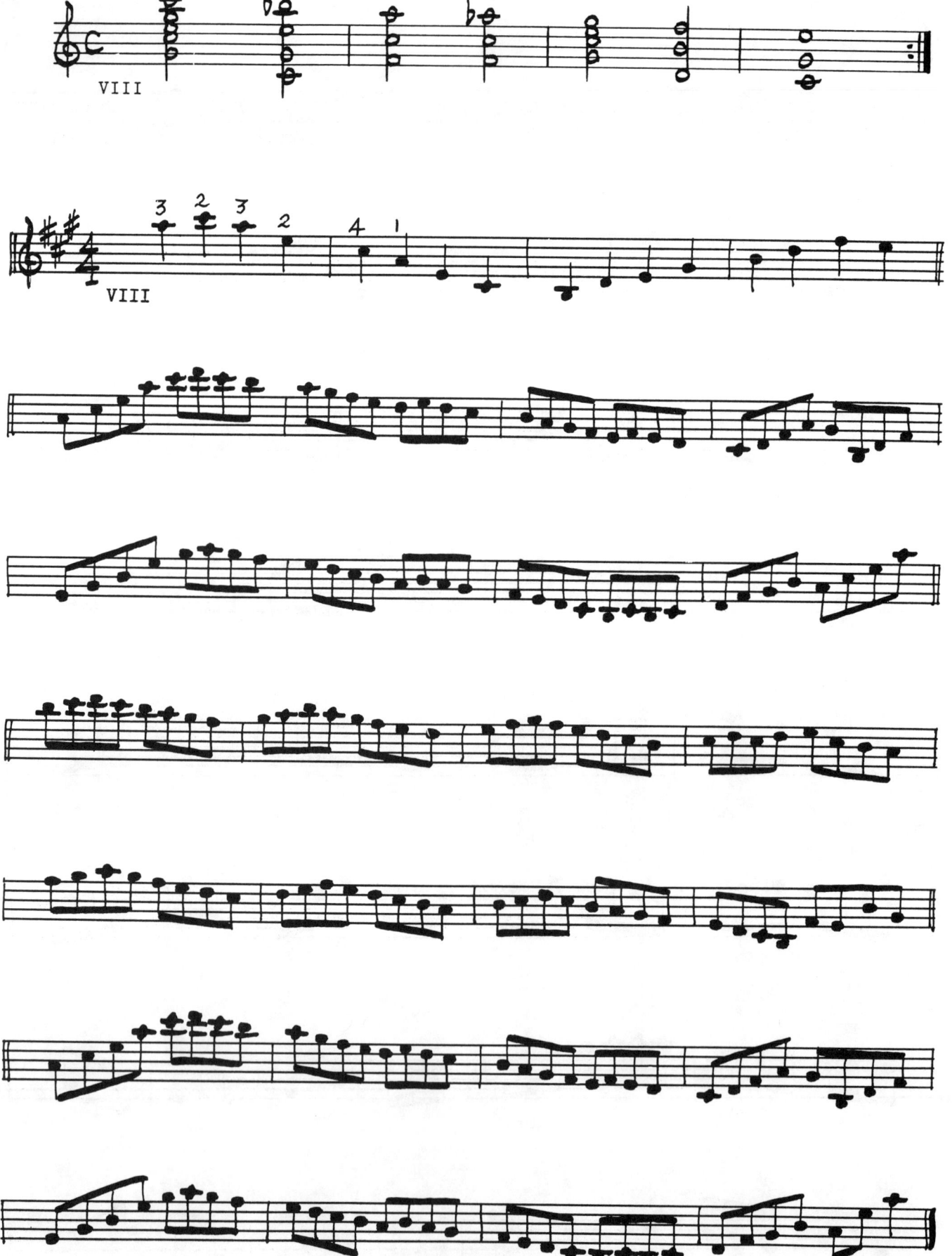

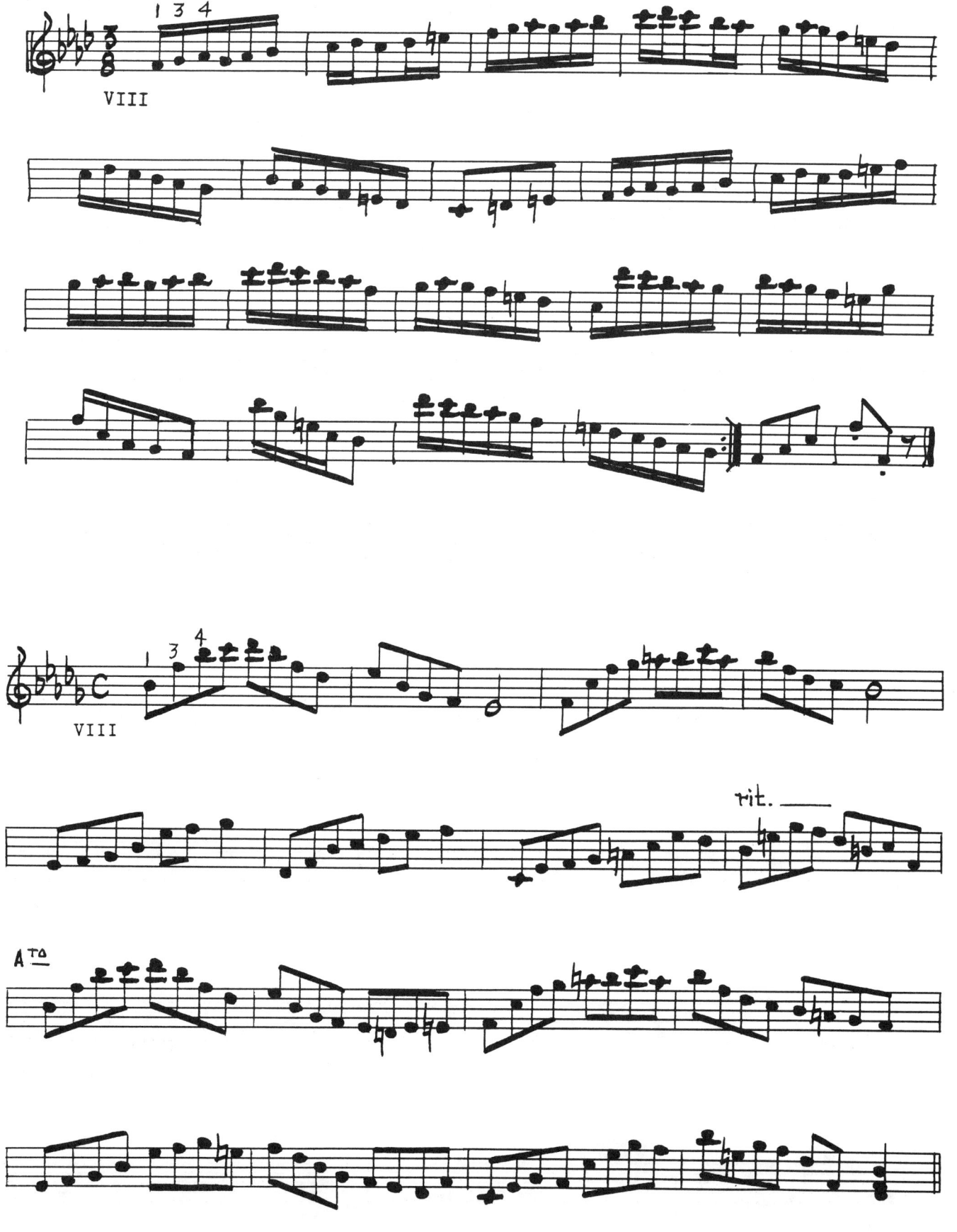

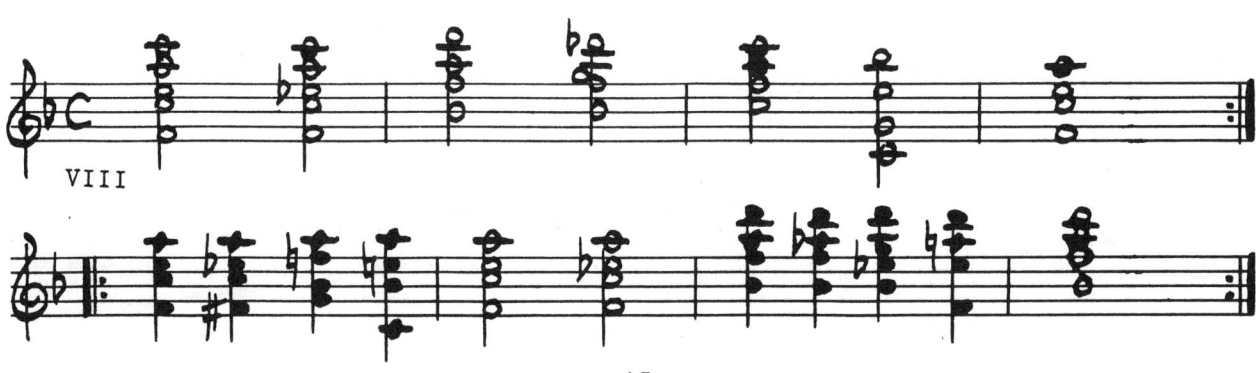

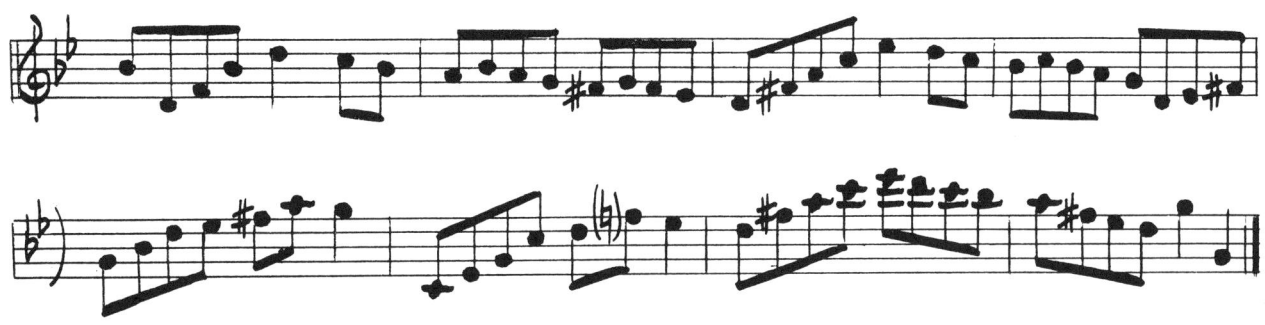

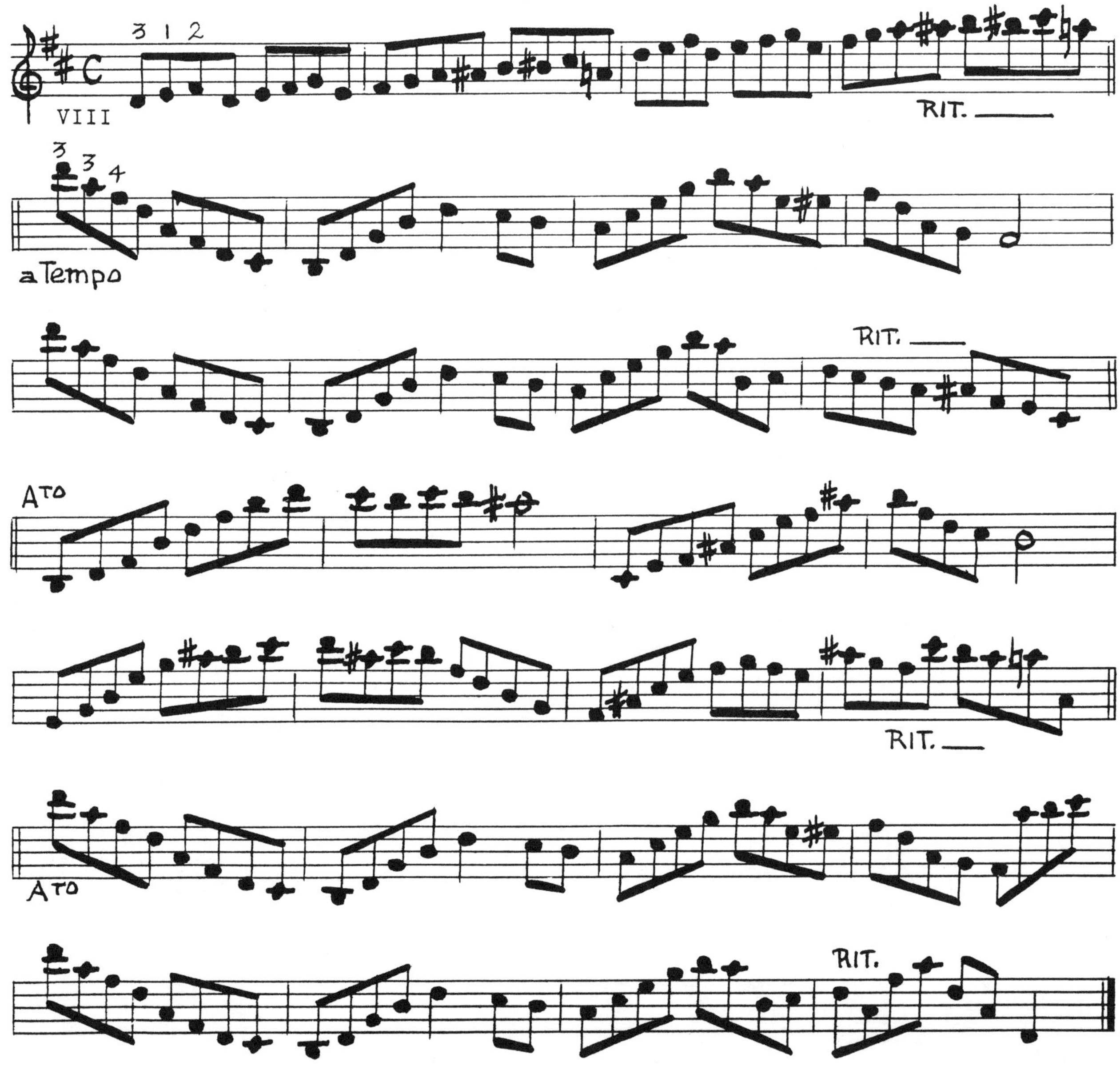
3 1 2
VIII
RIT.
3 3 4
a Tempo
RIT.
ATo
RIT.
ATo
RIT.

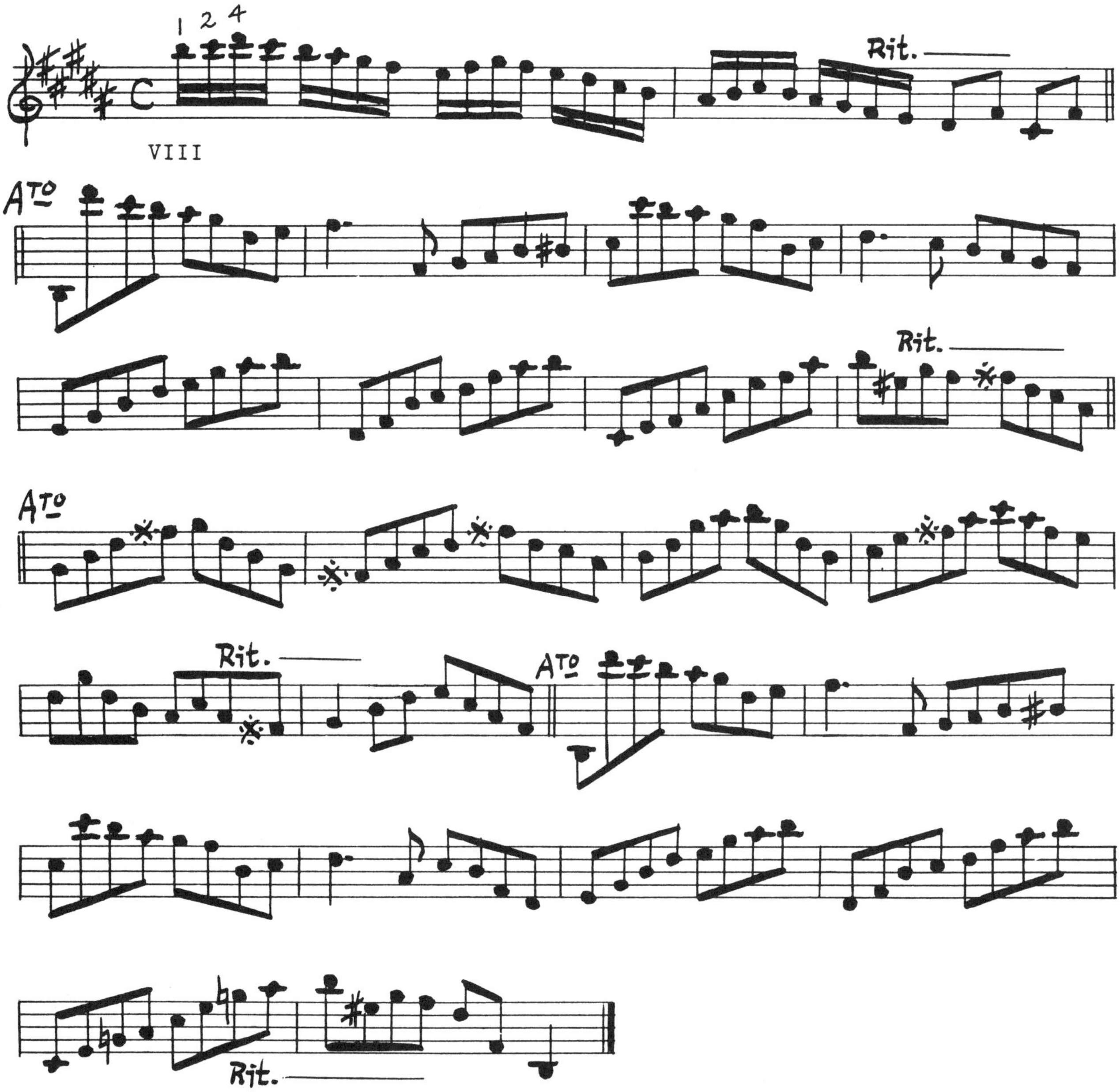
1 2 4
VIII
Rit.
Ato
Rit.
Ato
Rit.
Ato
Rit.

4 3 4 2 4
VIII
rit.

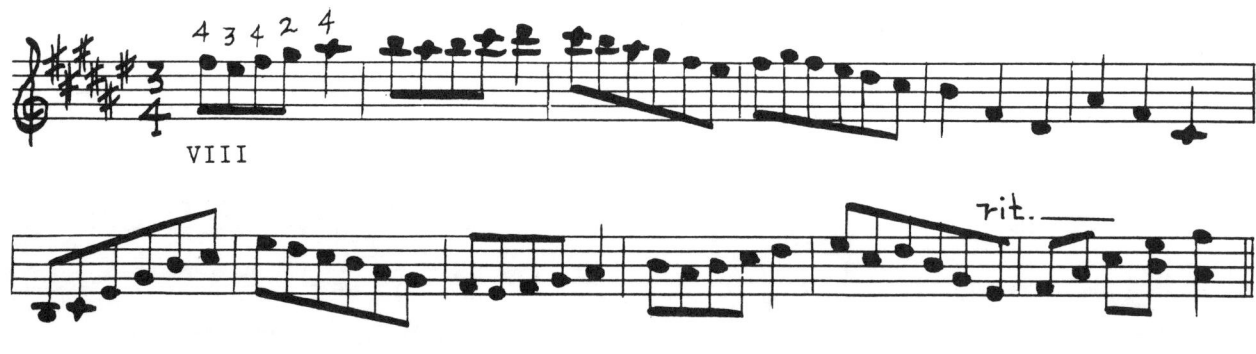

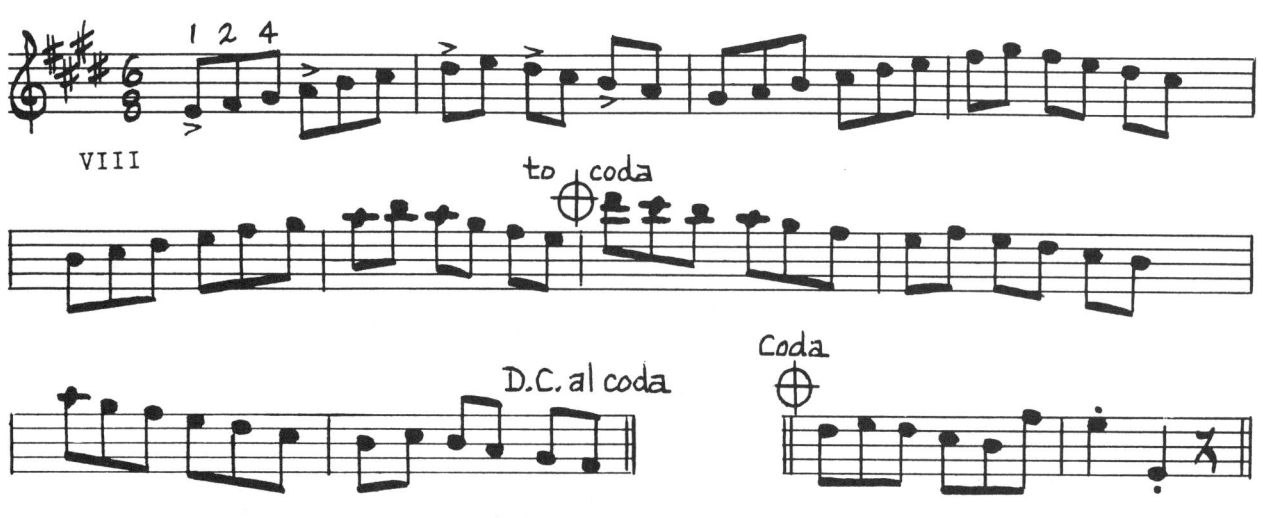
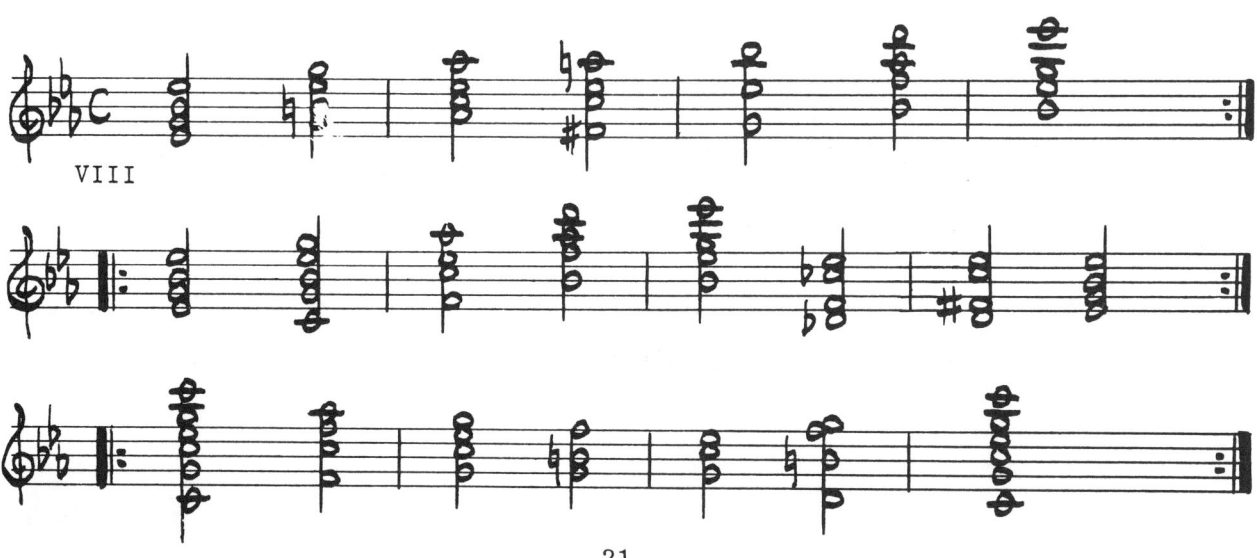

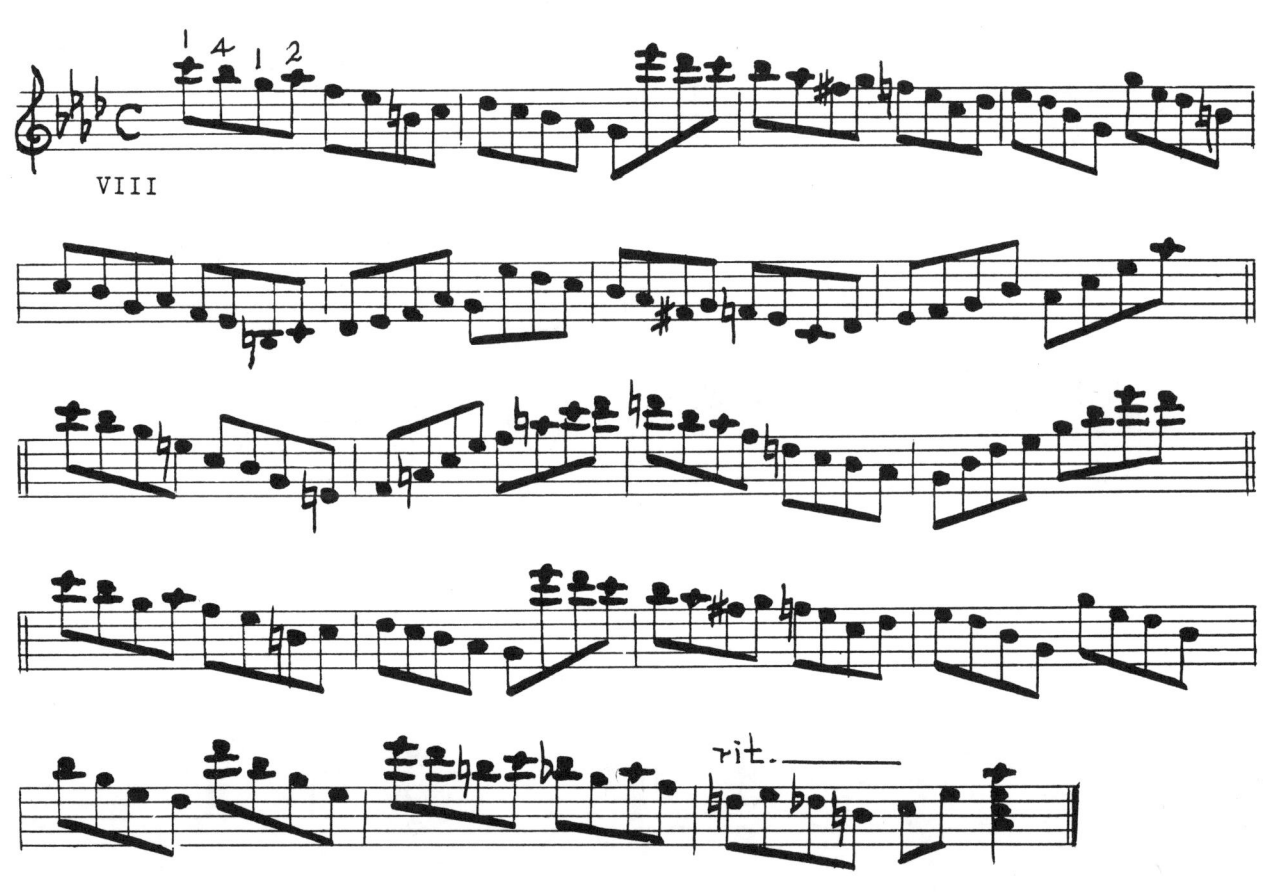

23

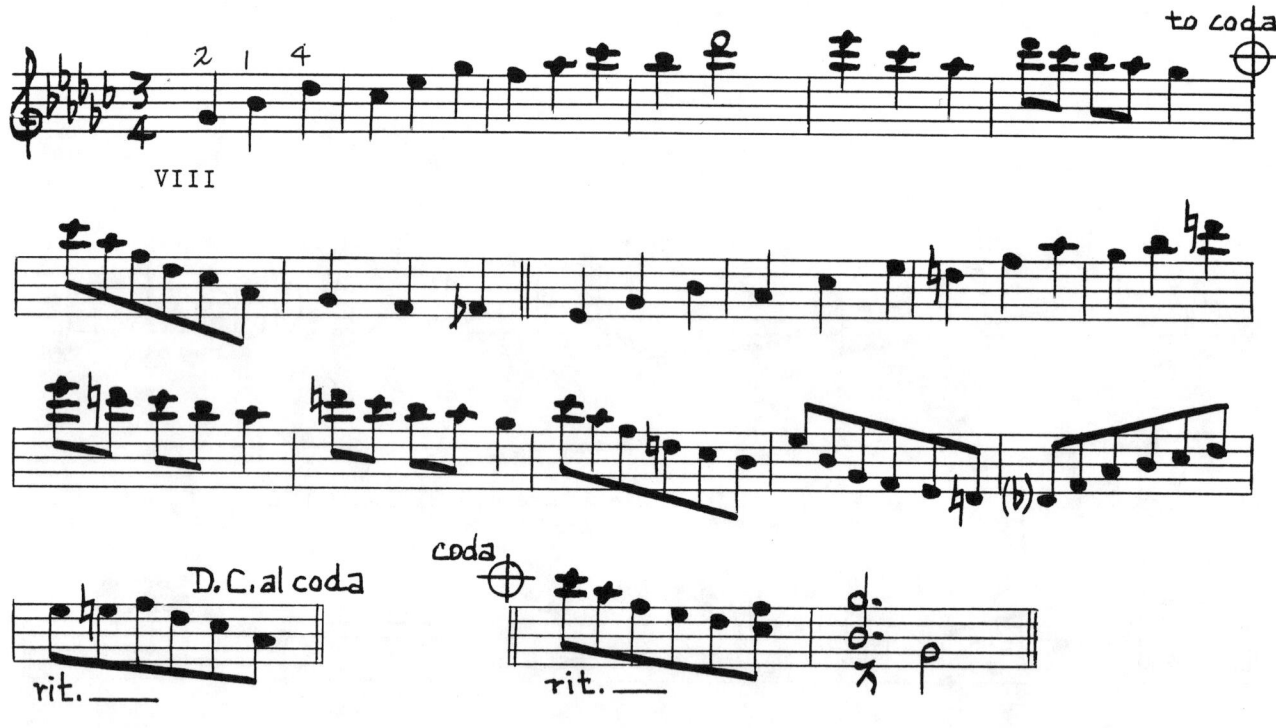

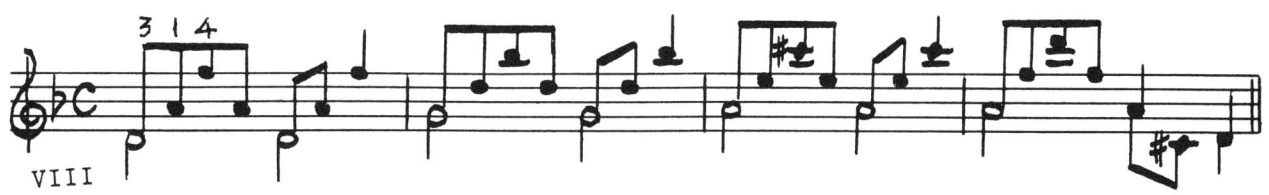

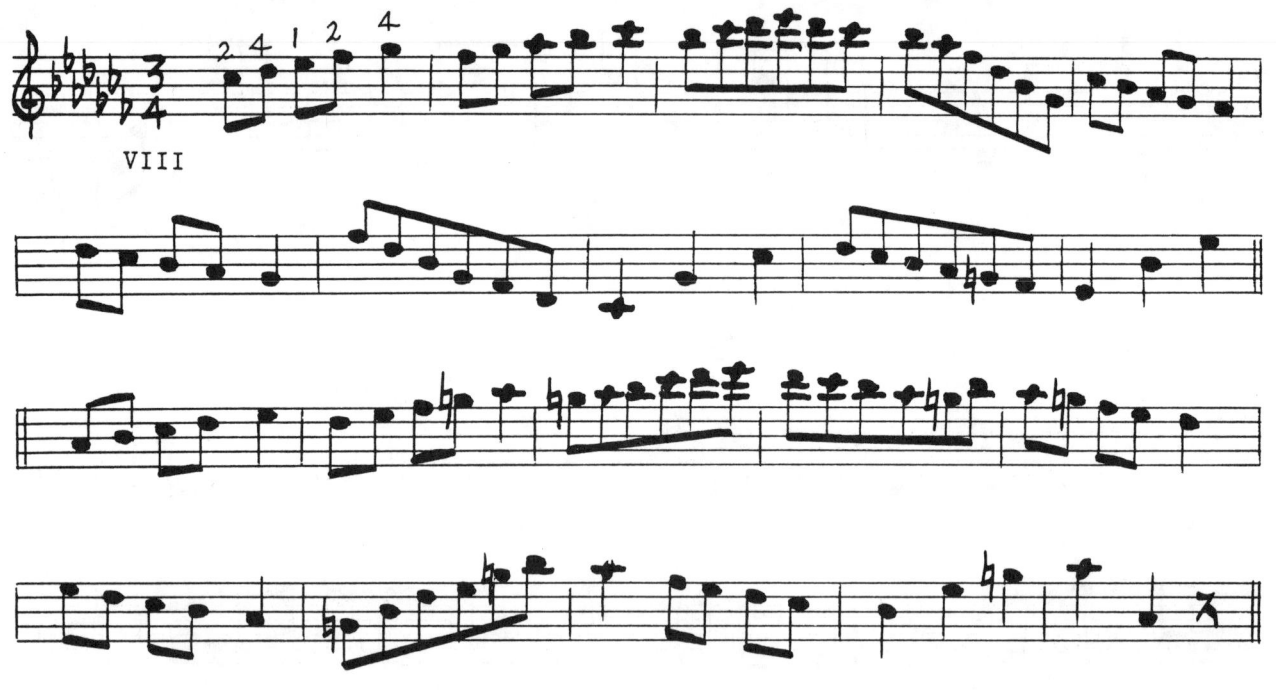
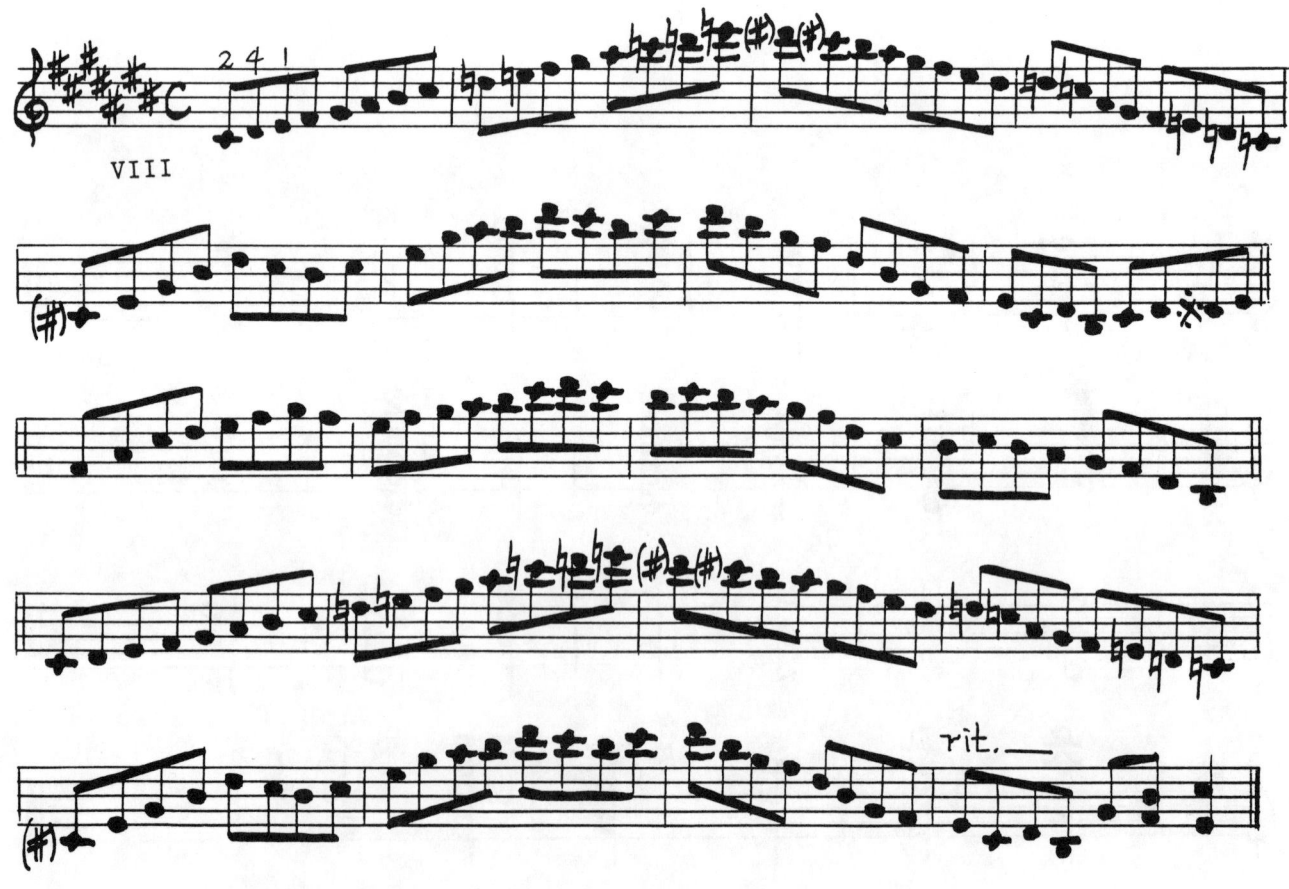

## 9th POSITION

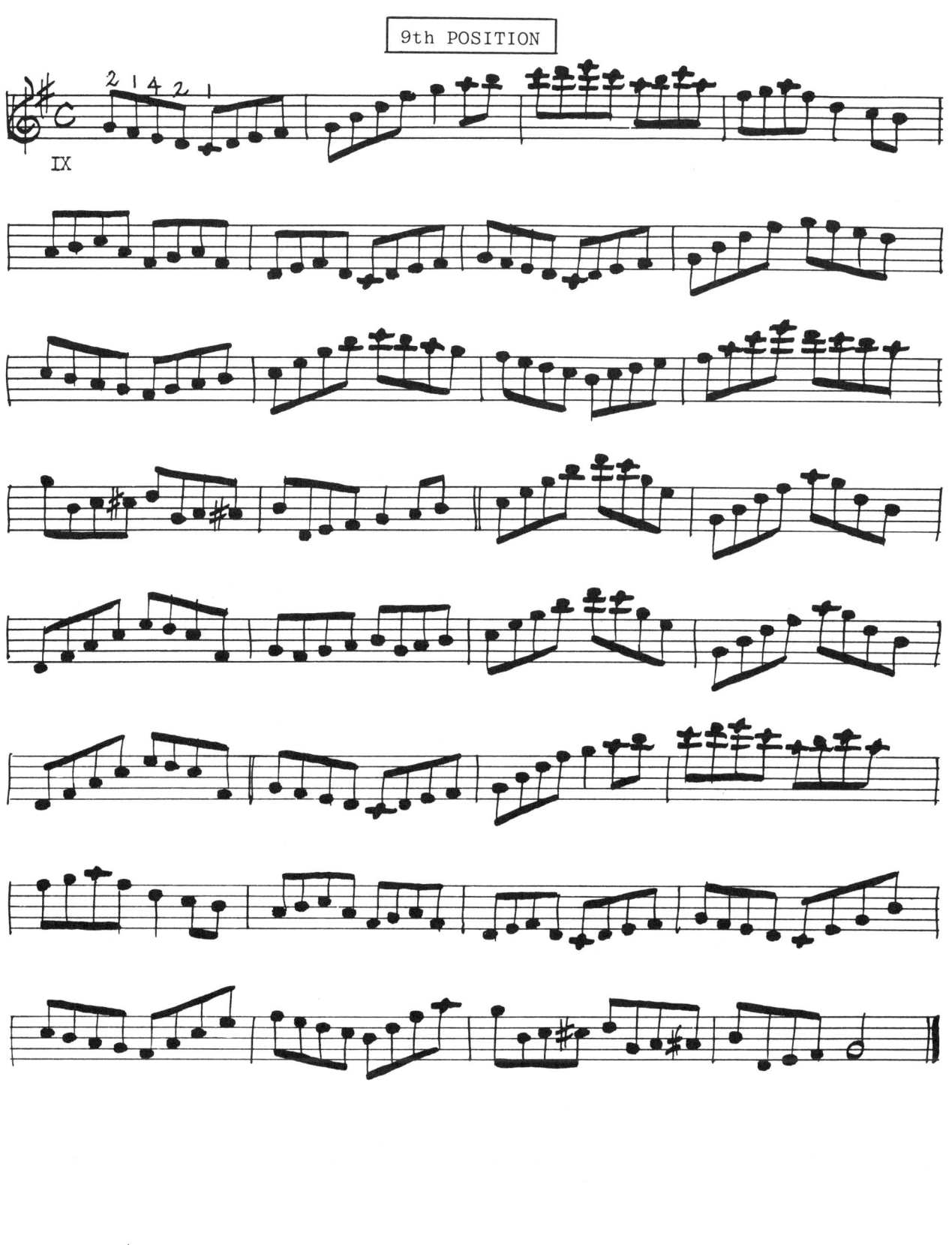

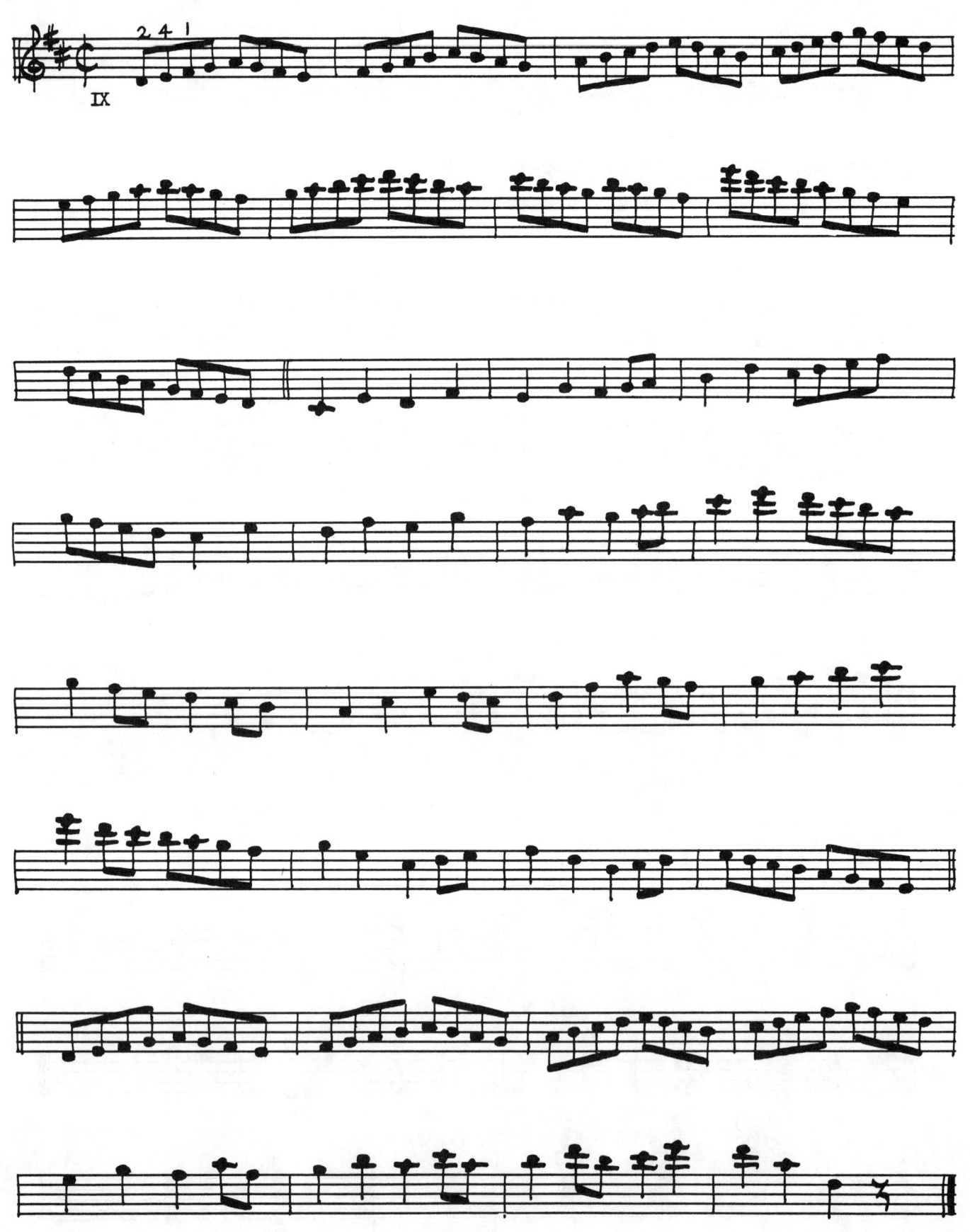

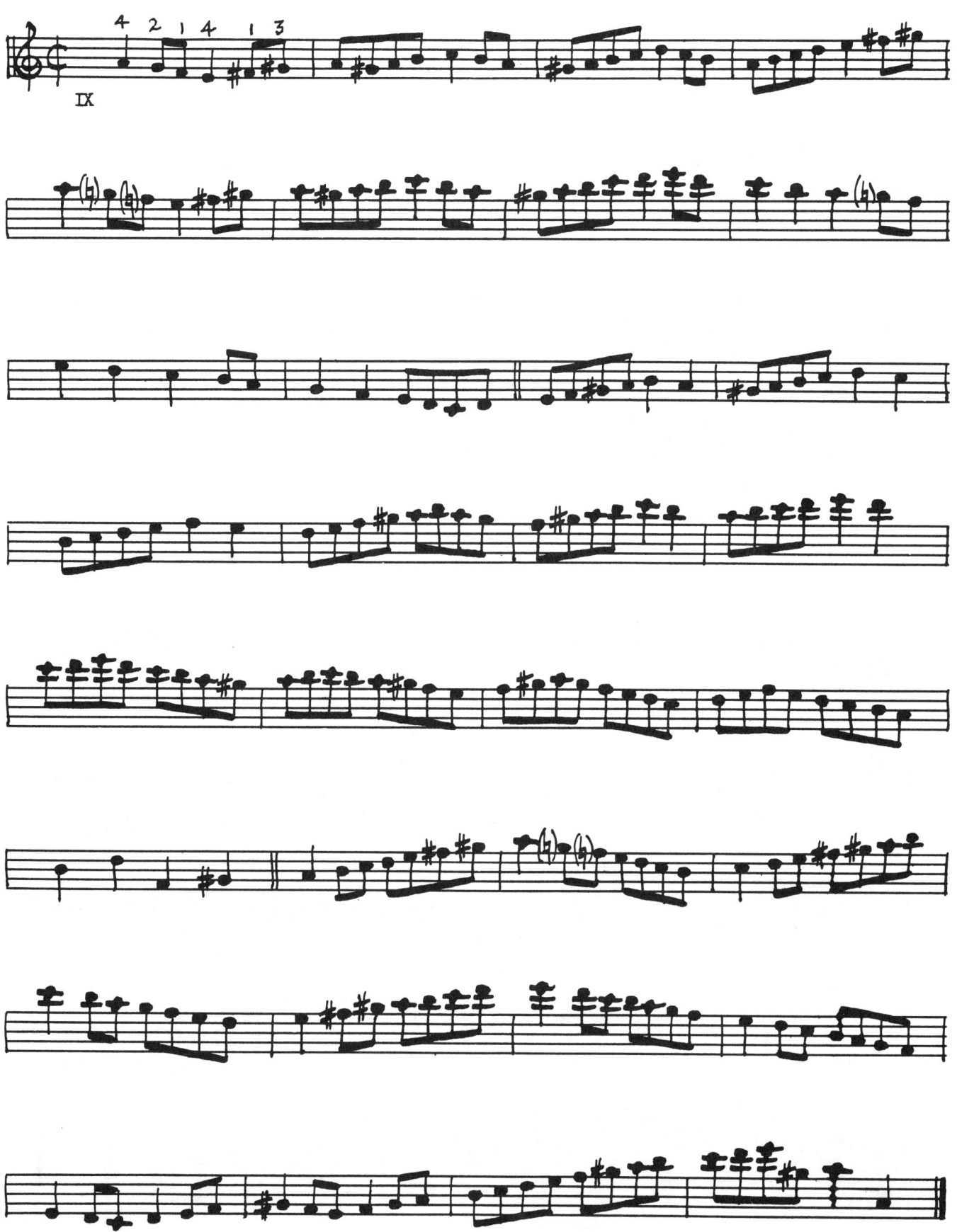

33

34

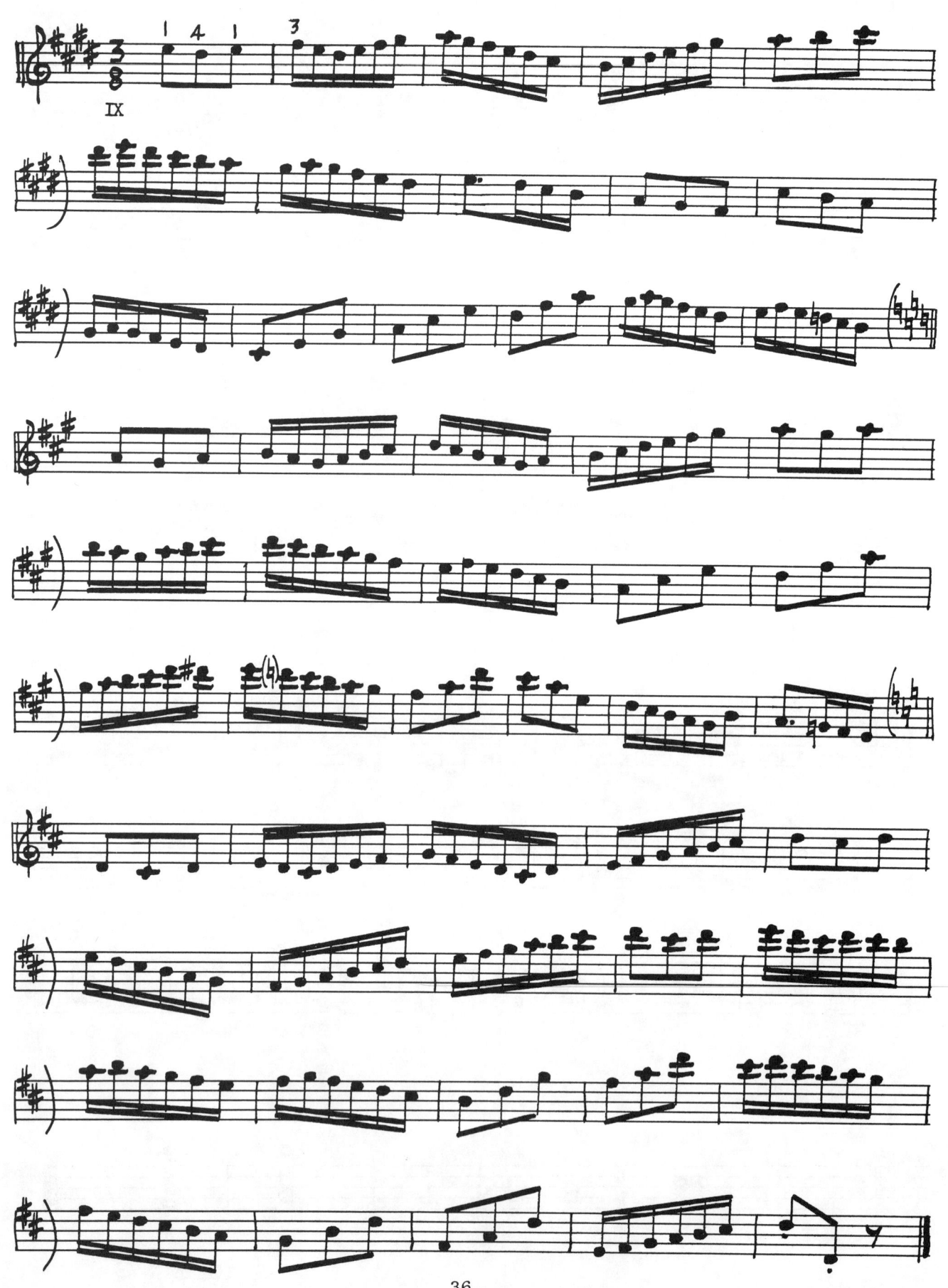

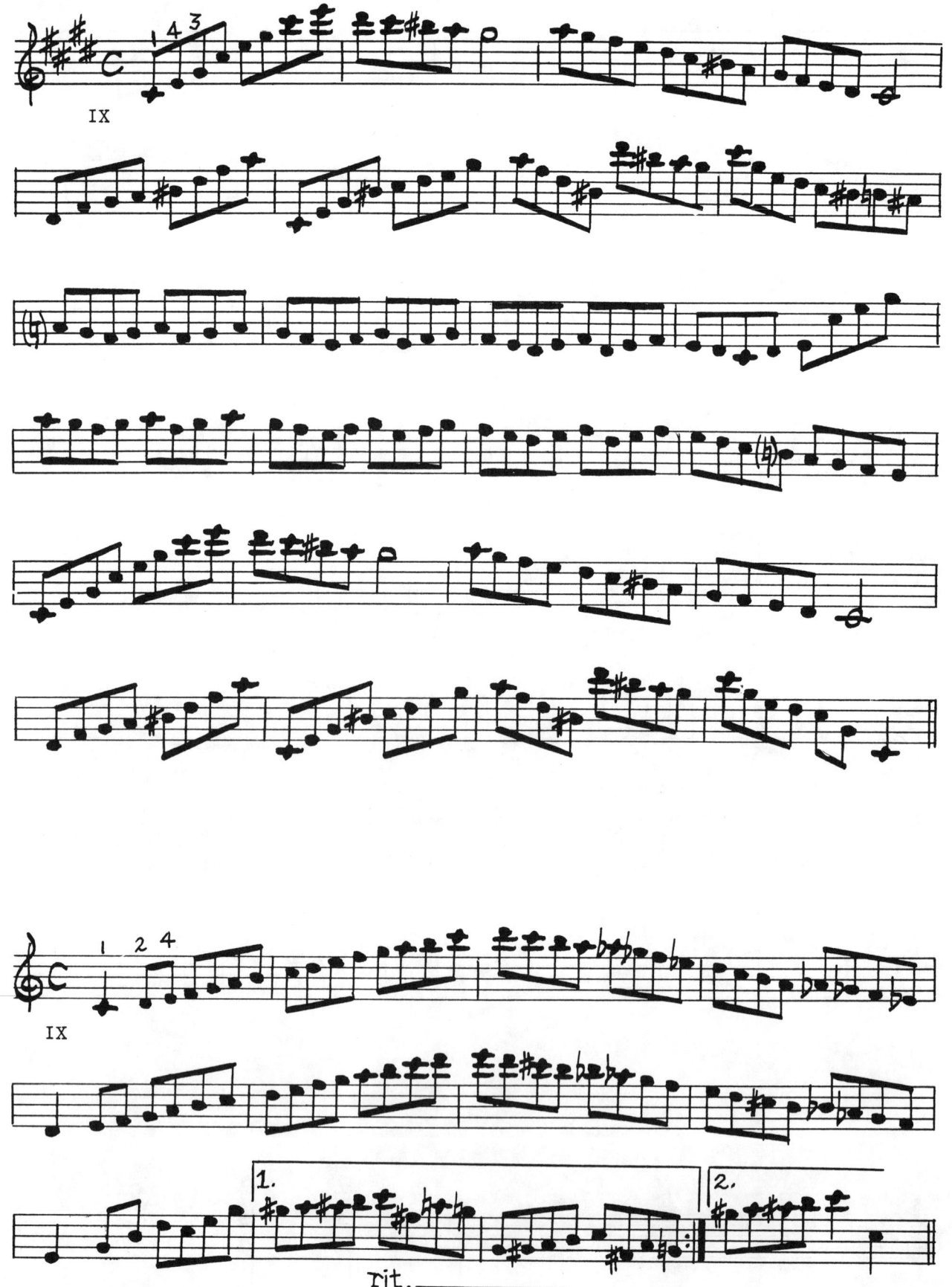

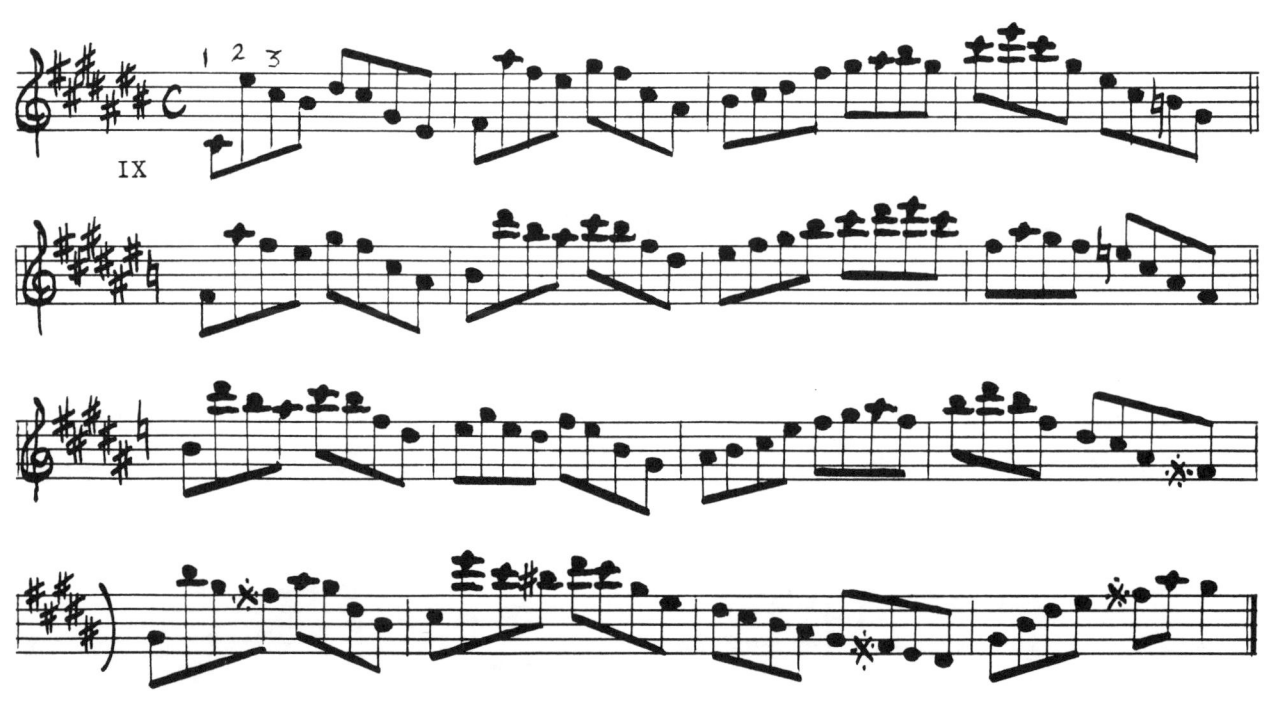

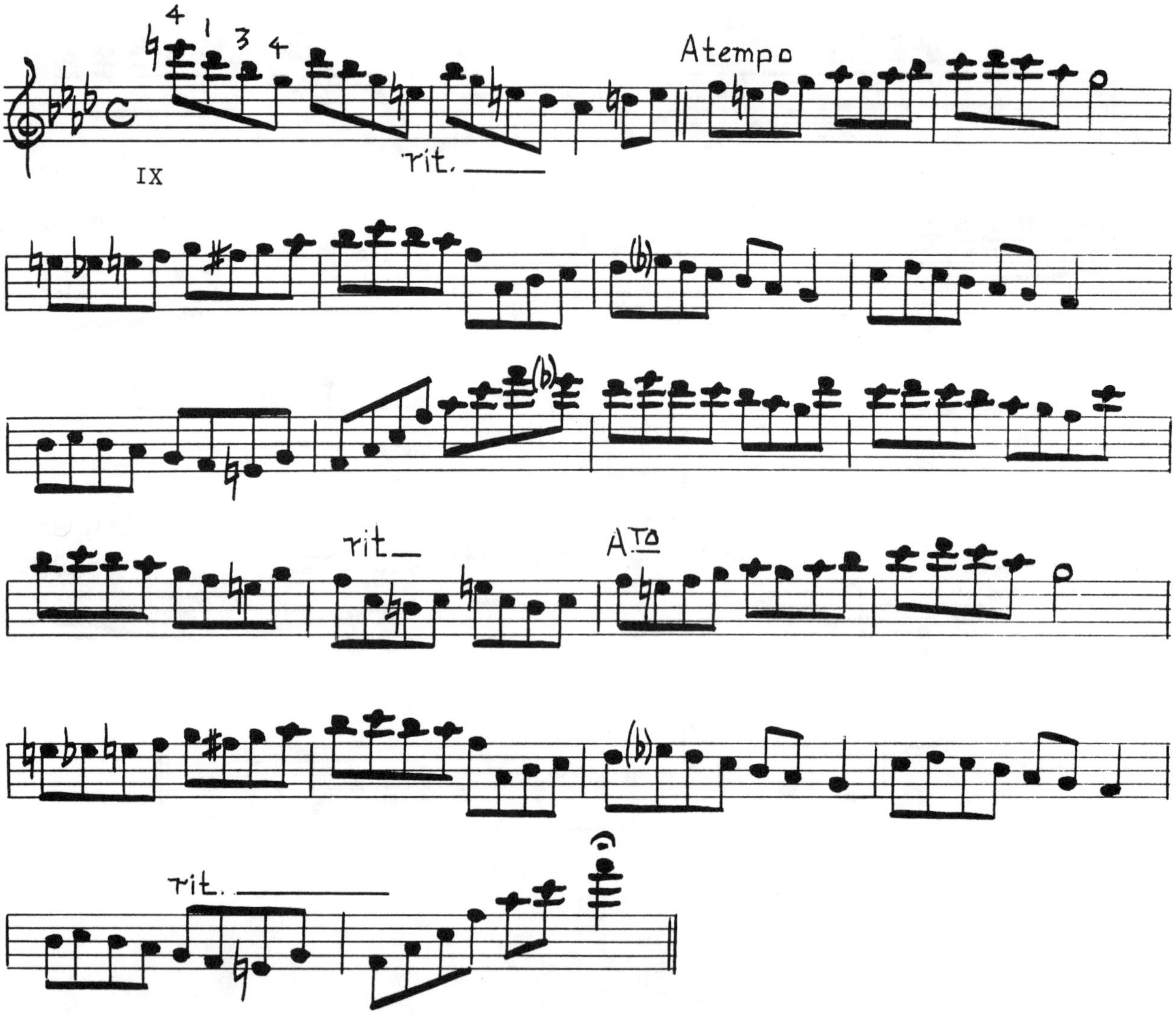
4 1 3 4
IX
rit.
Atempo
rit.
A To
rit.

4 3 2
IX

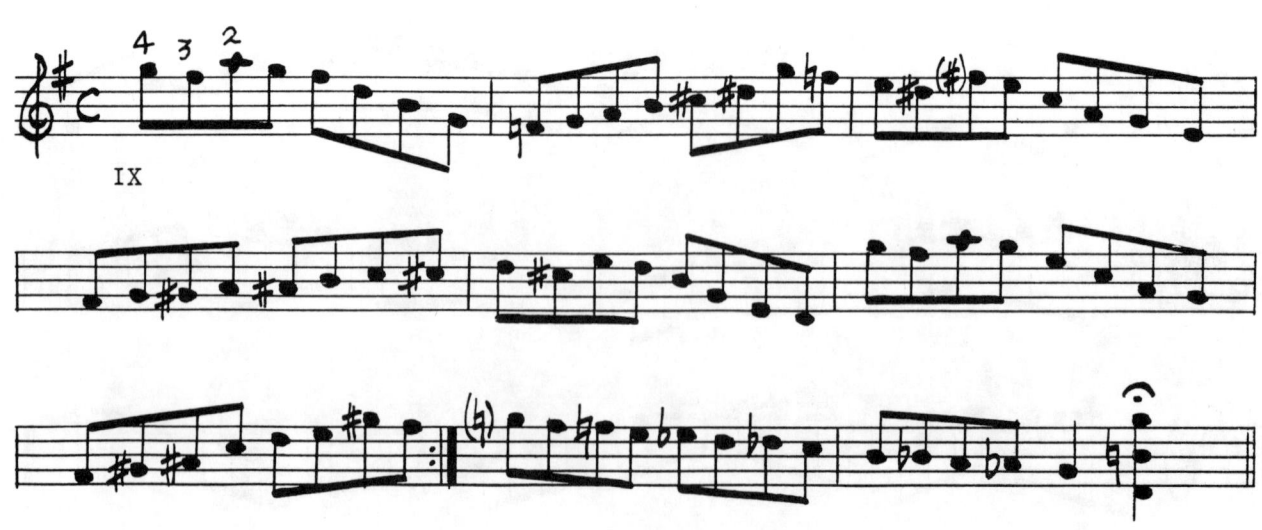

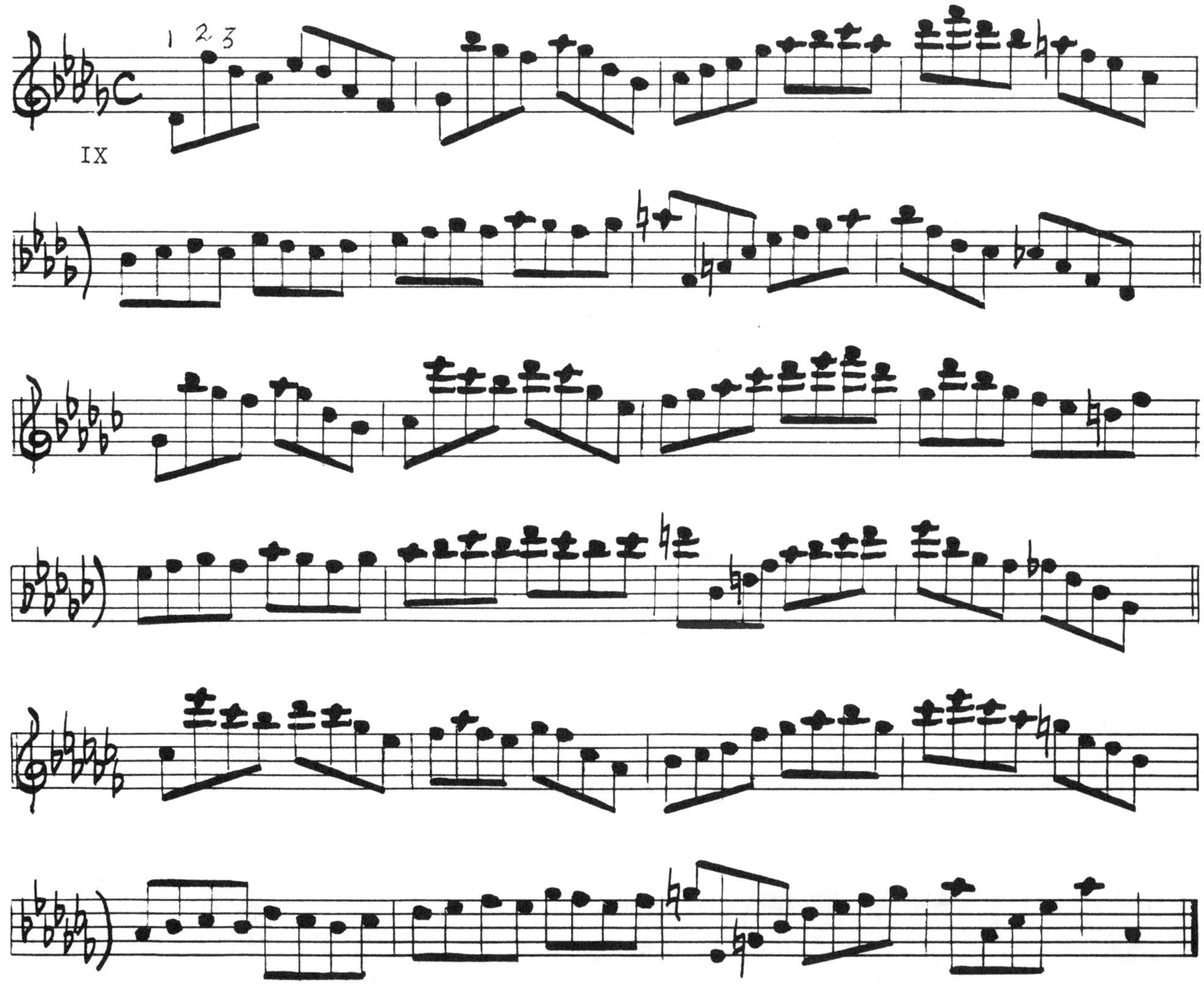

45

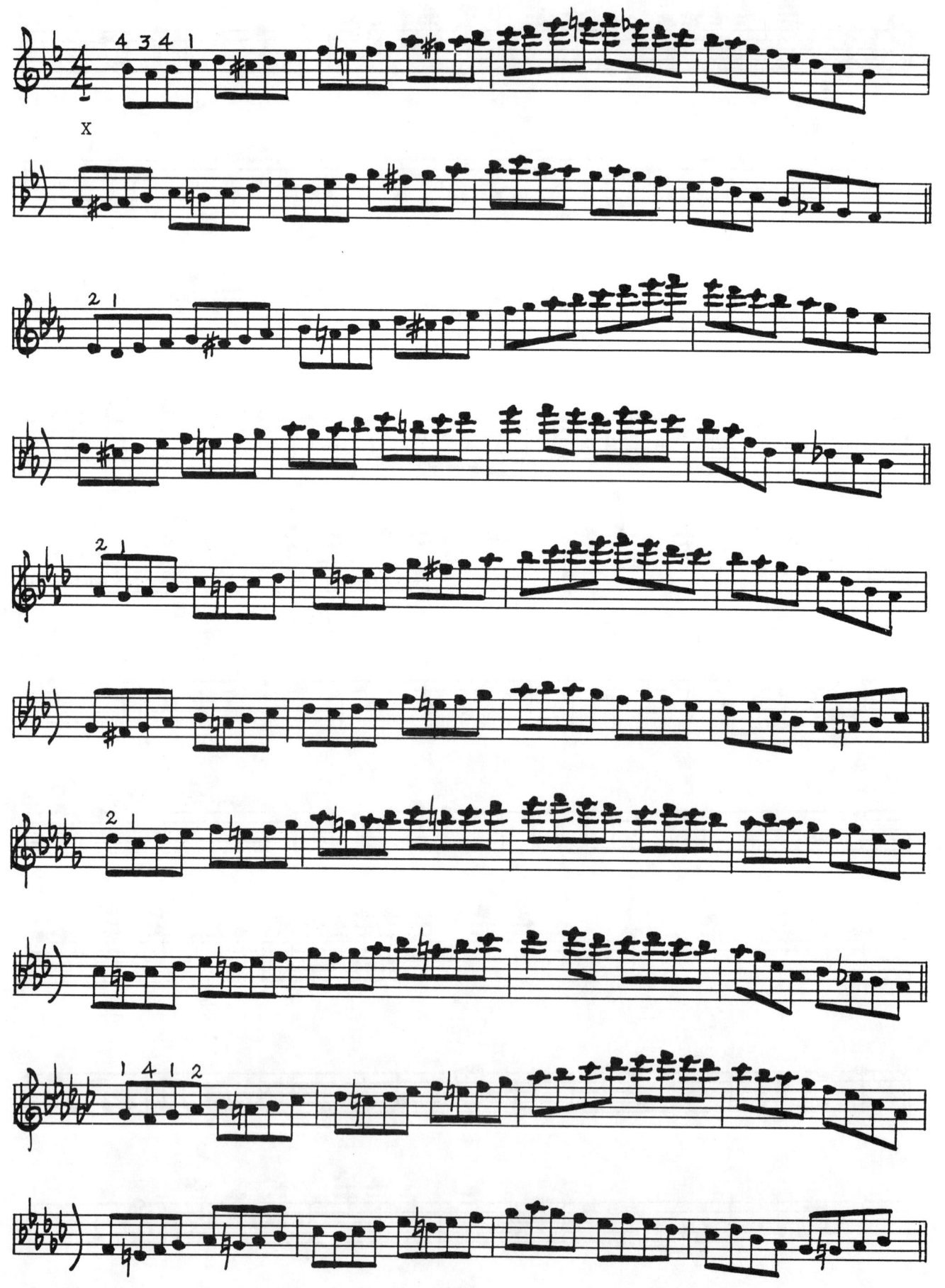

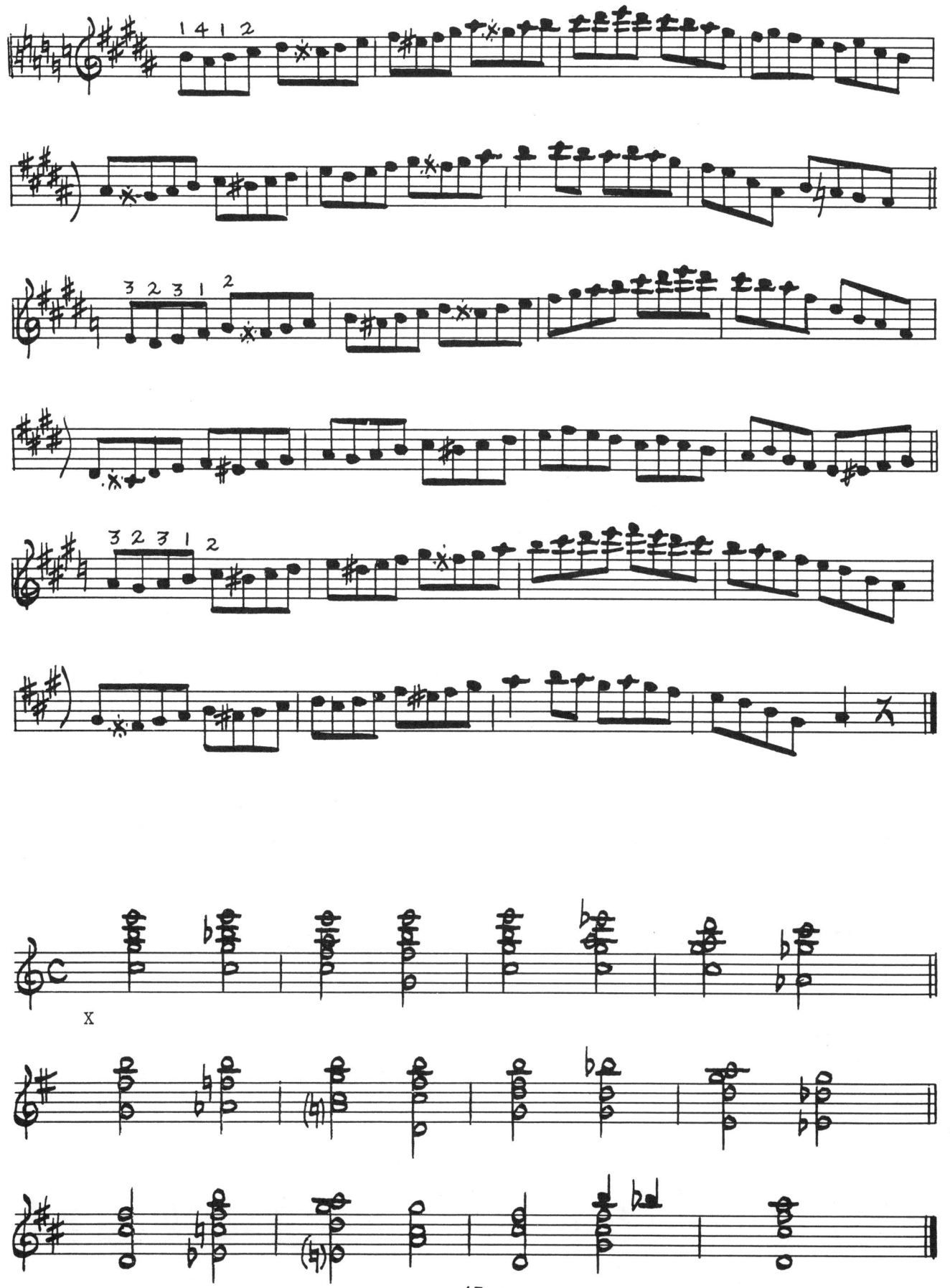

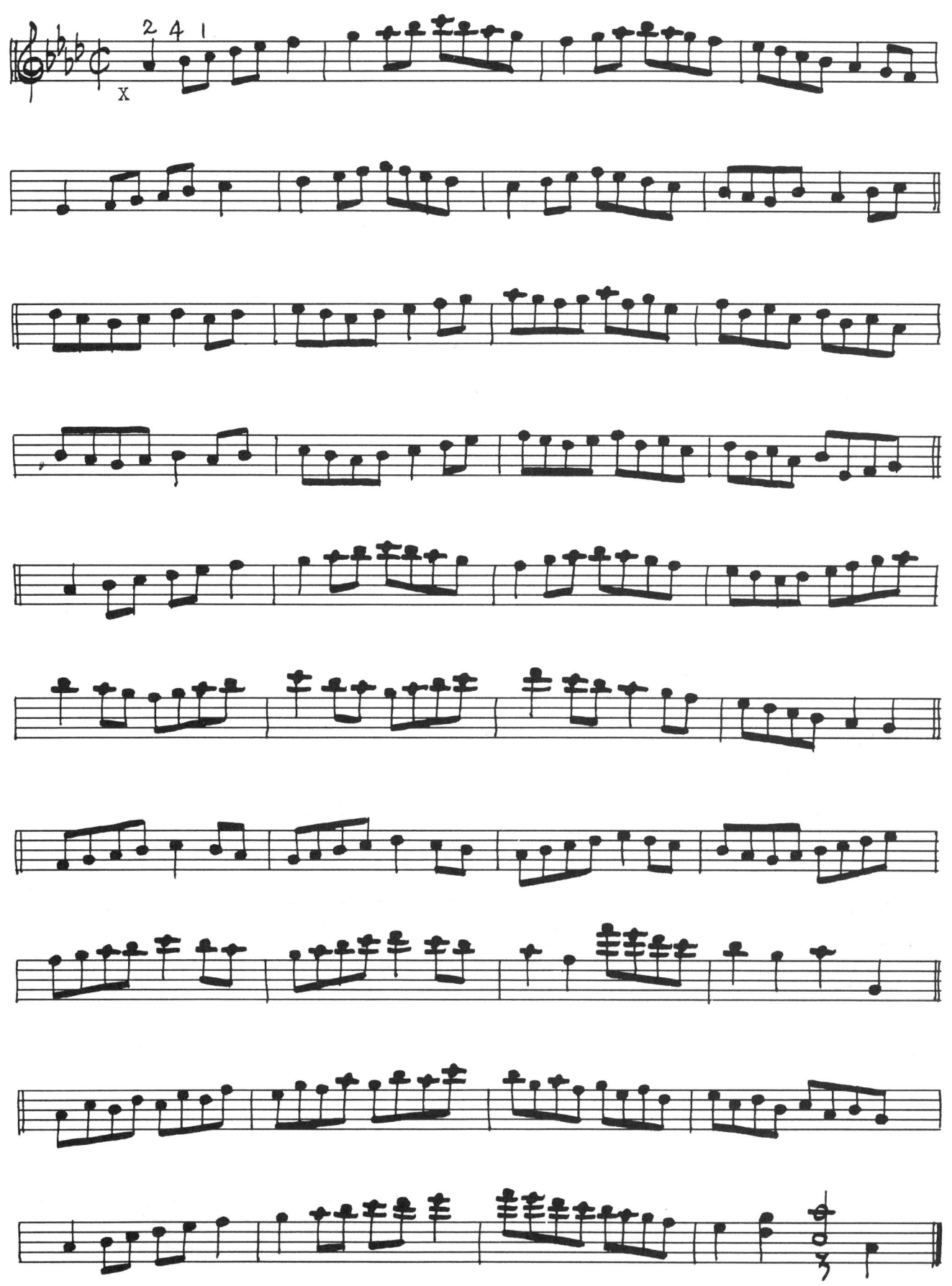

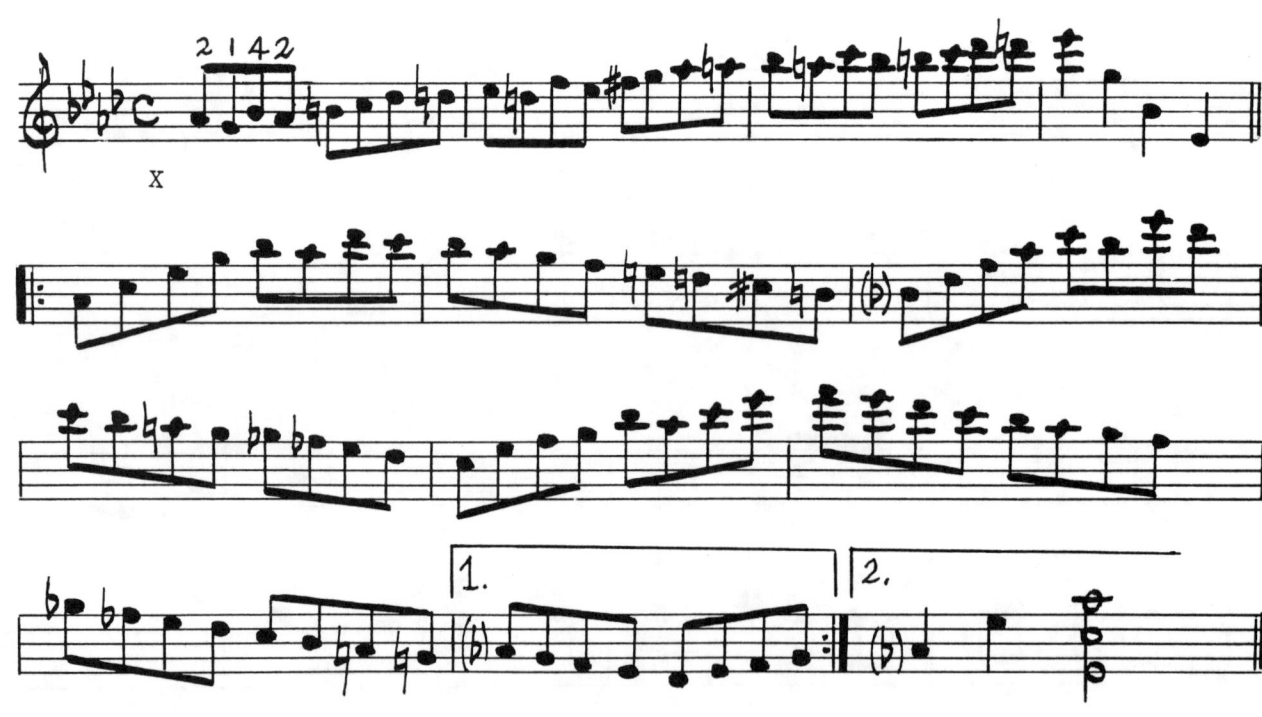

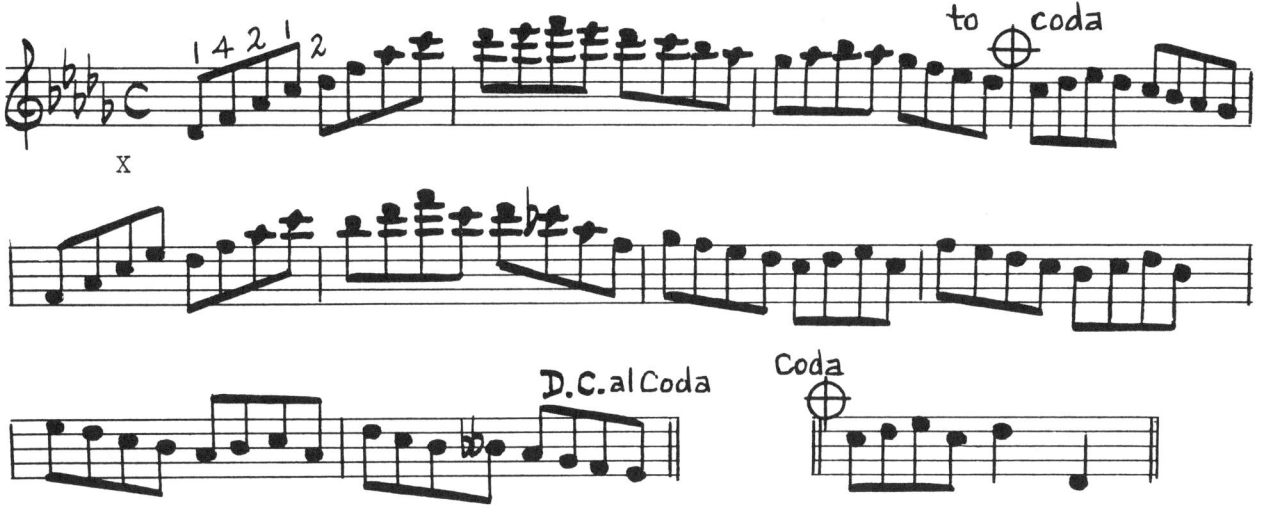

55

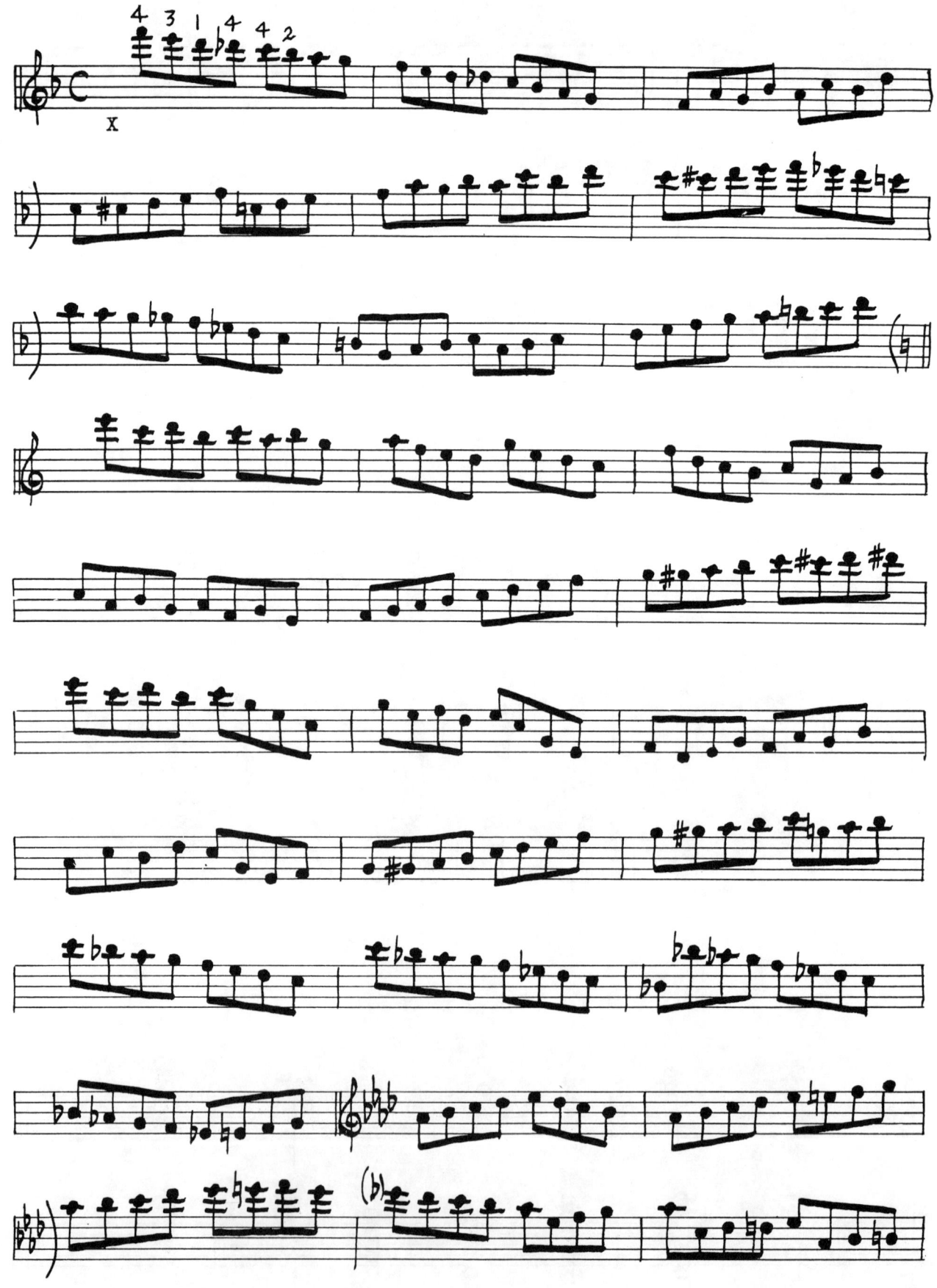

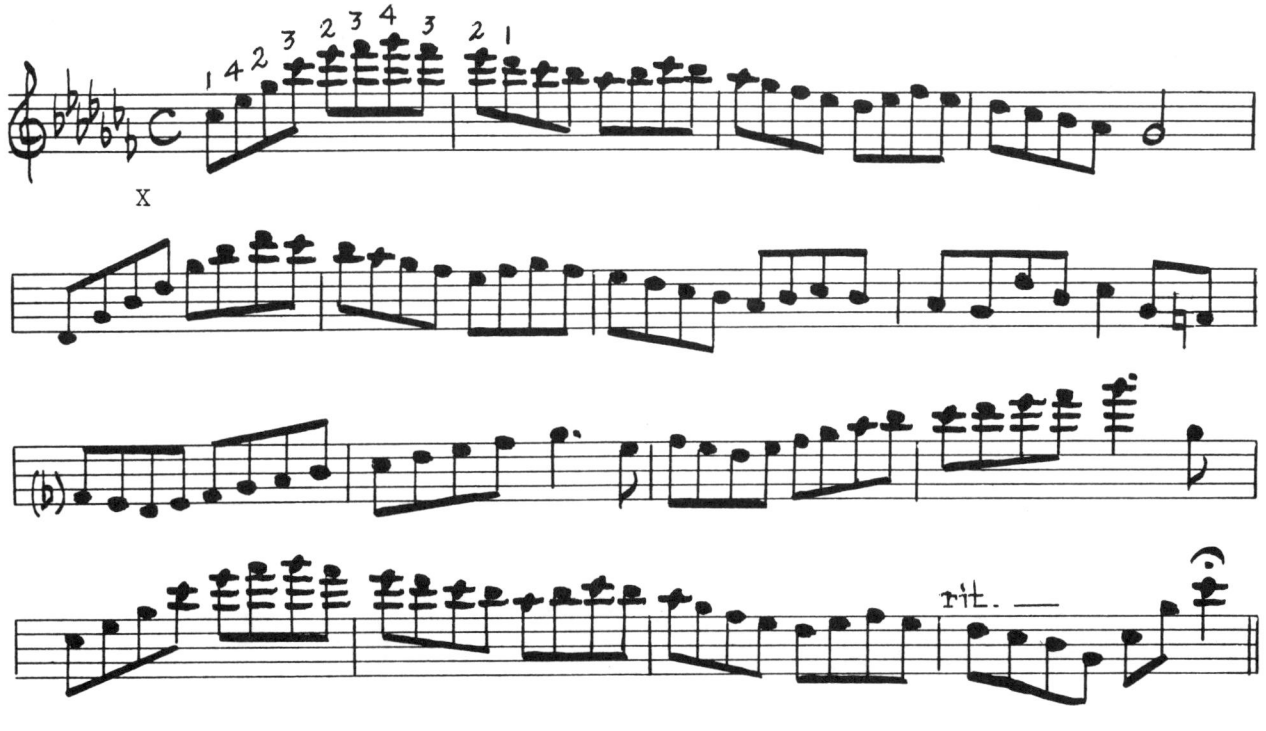

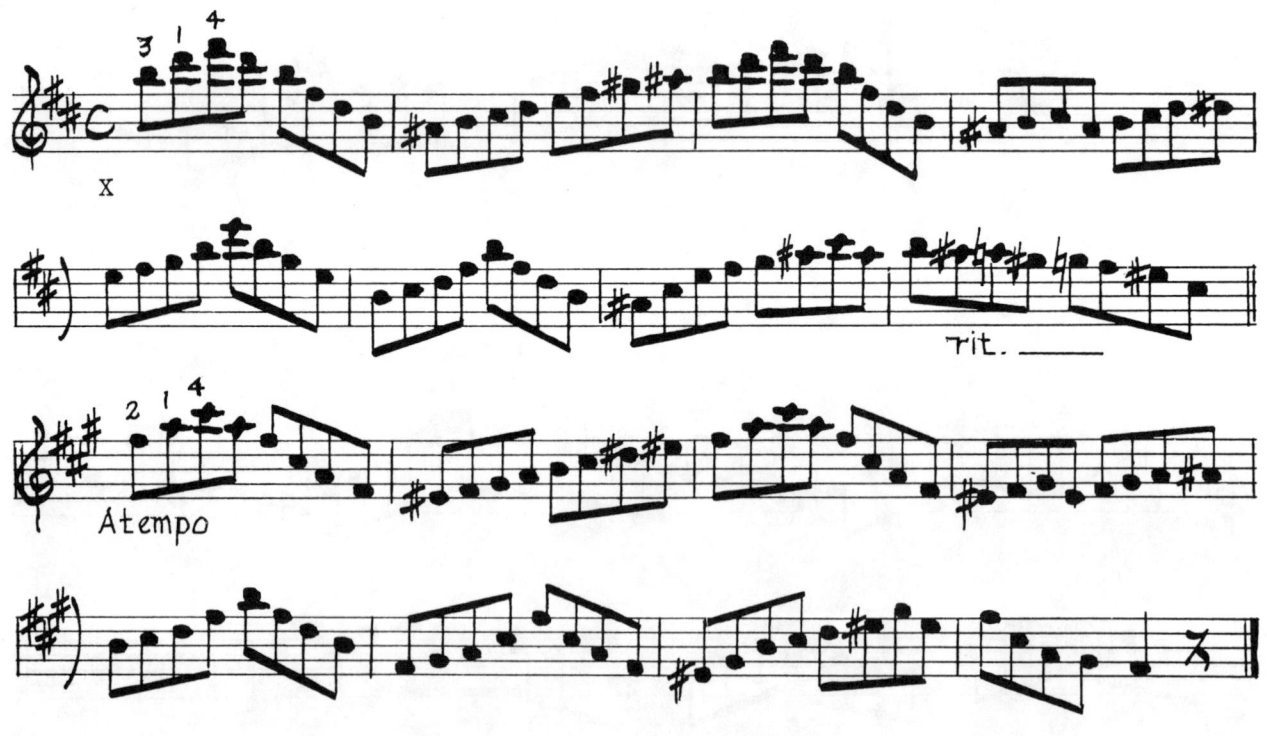

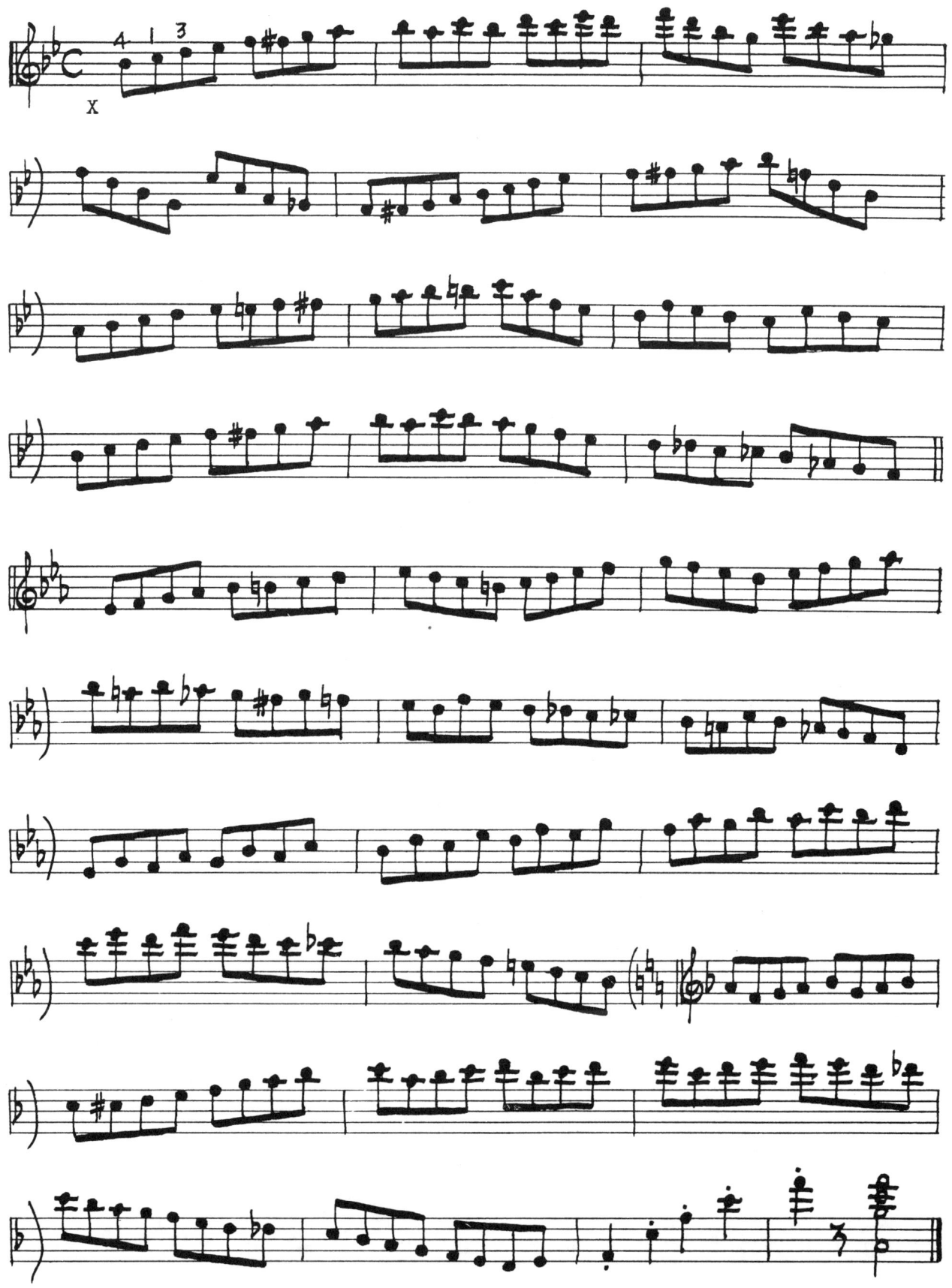

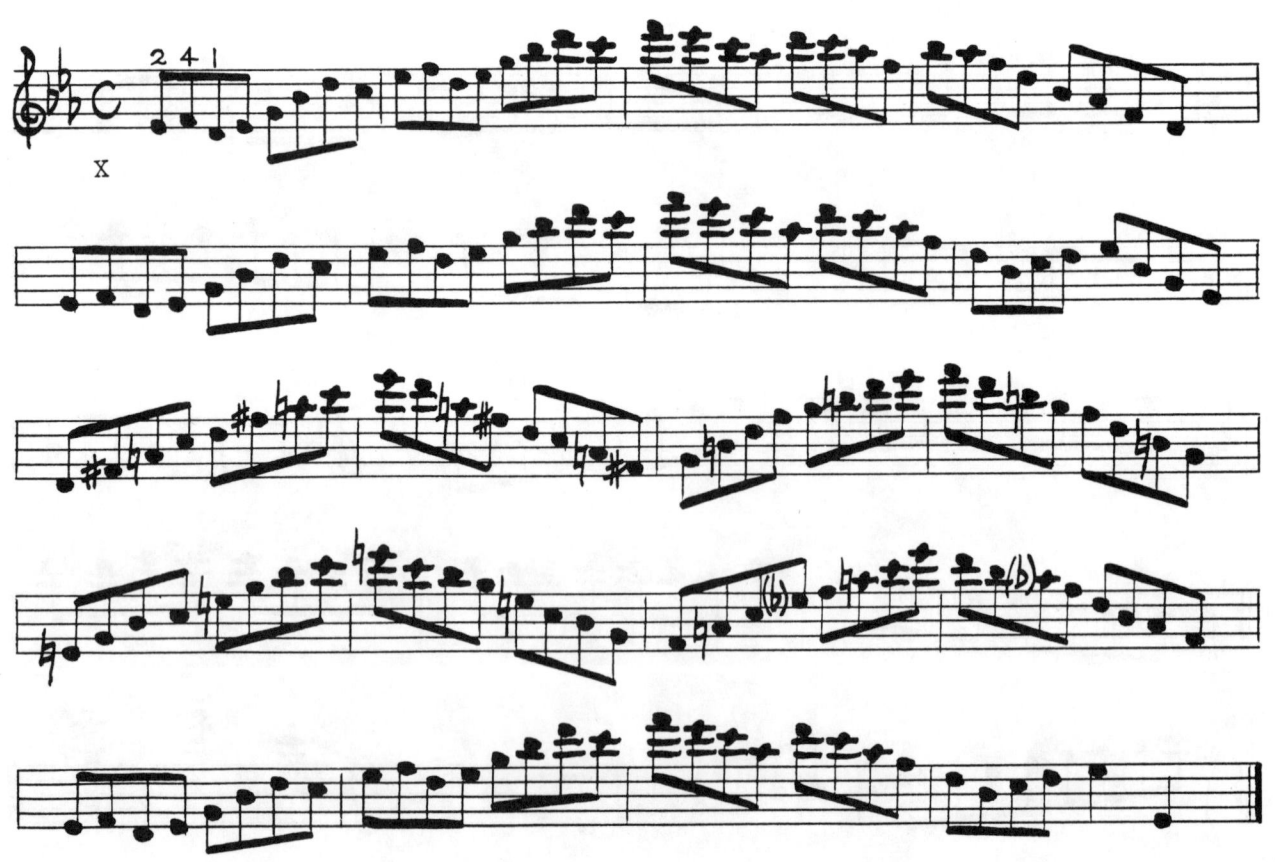

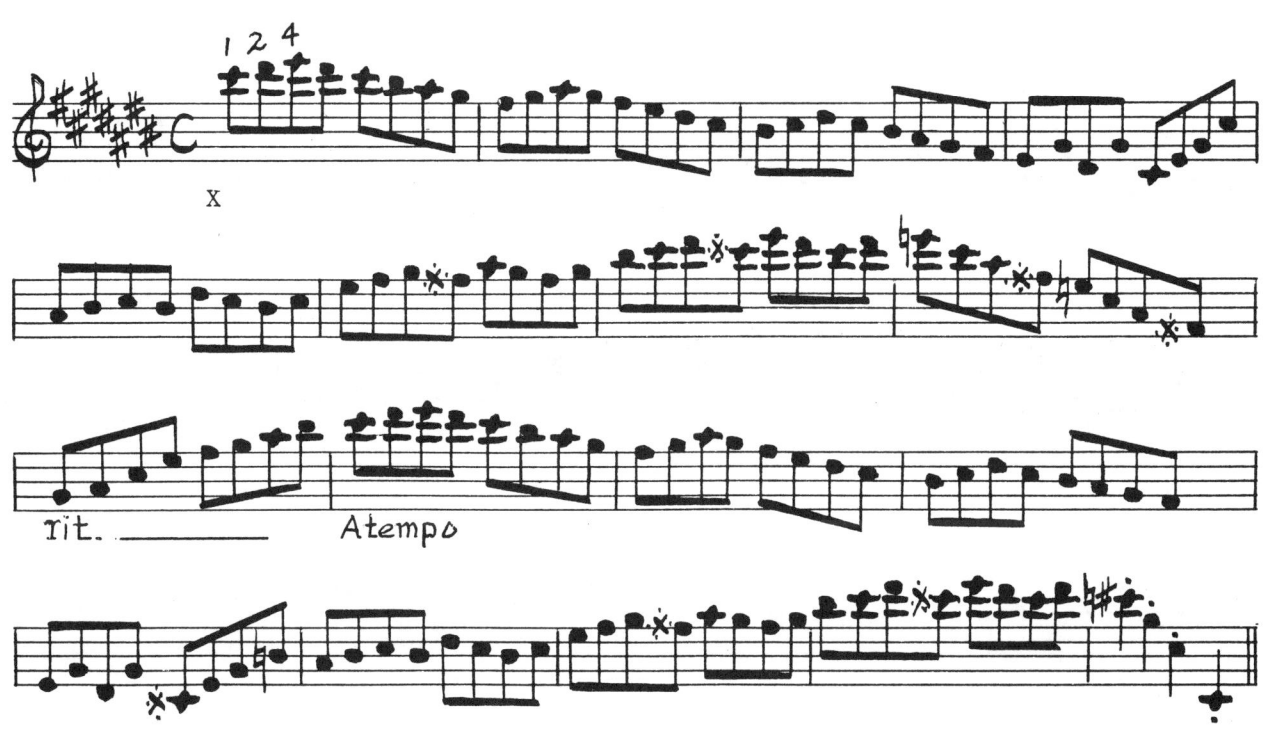

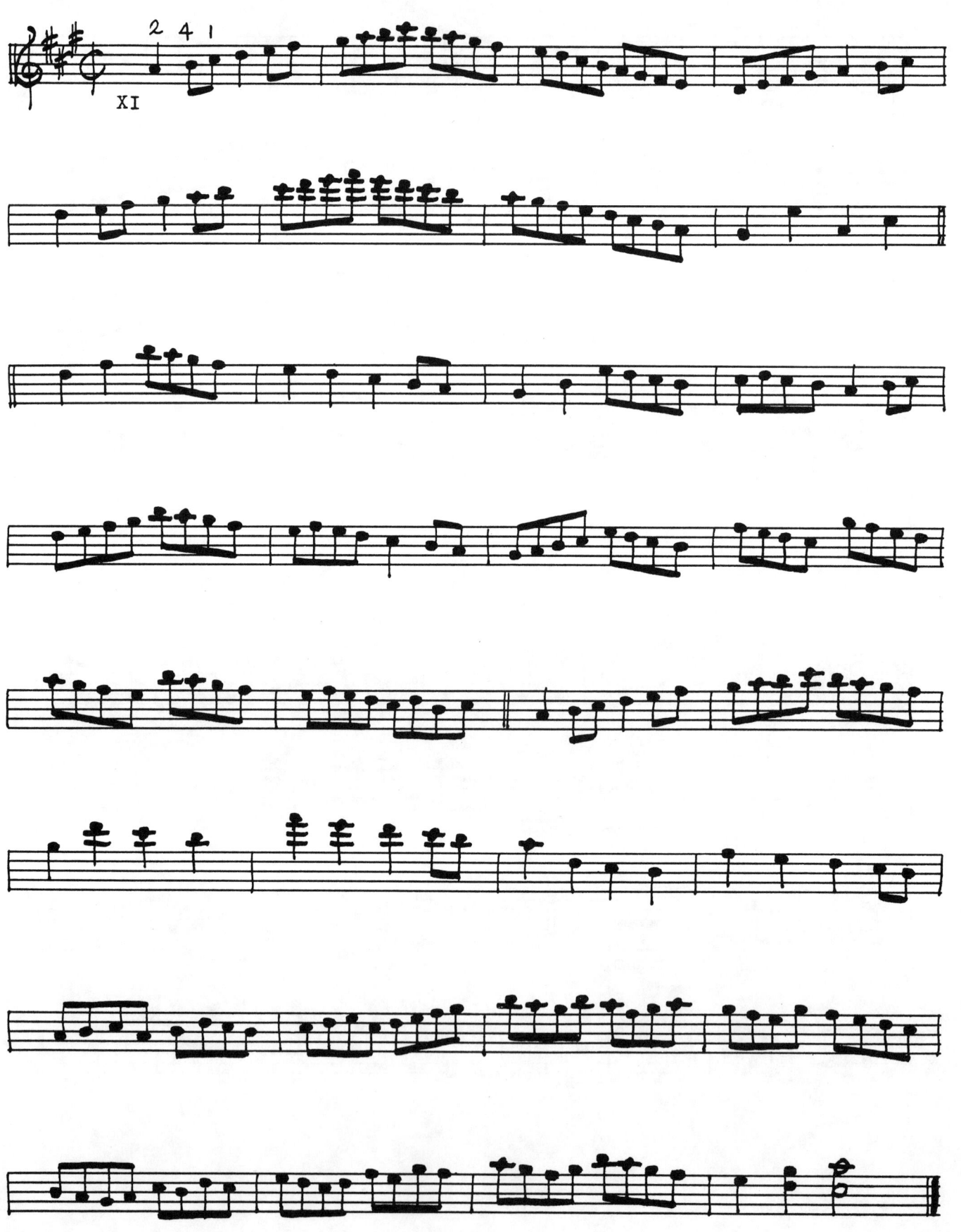

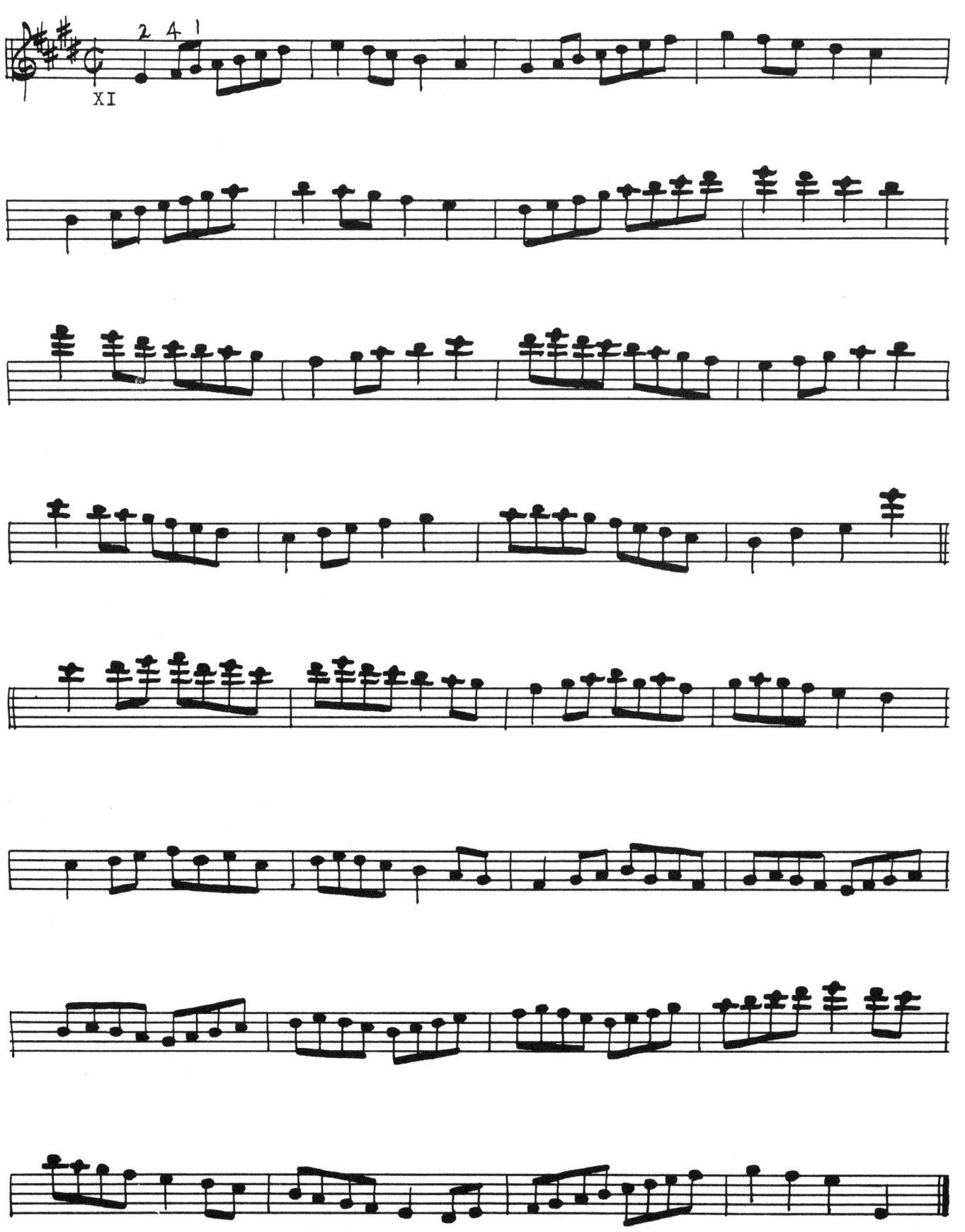

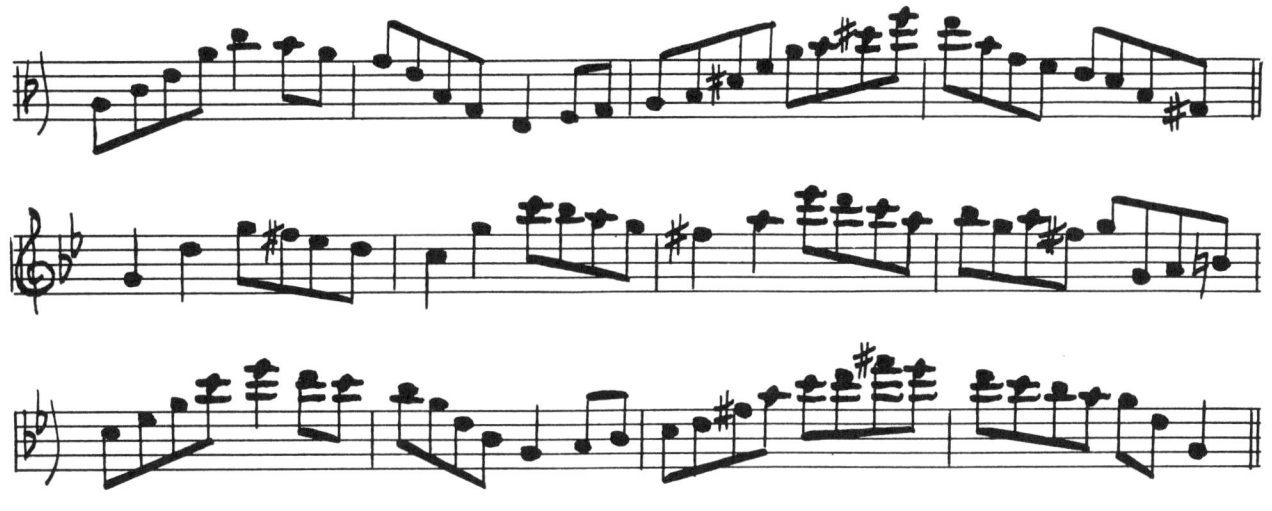

75

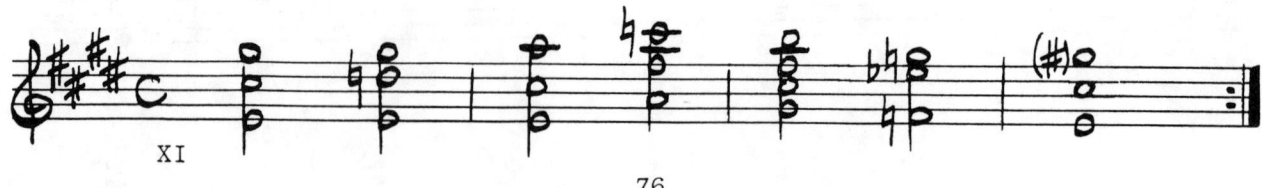

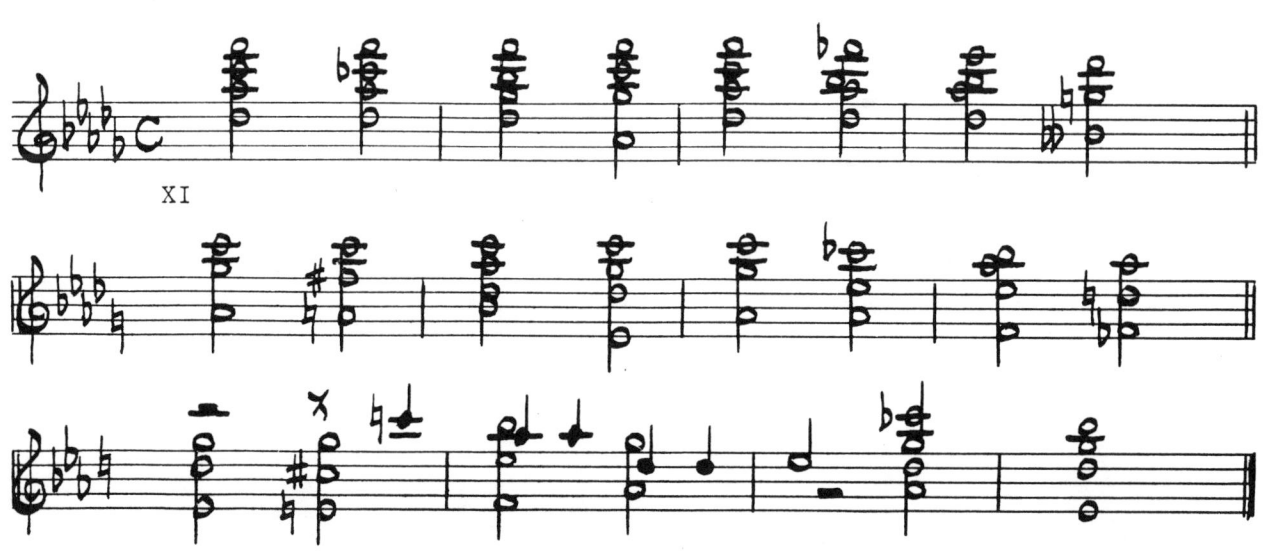

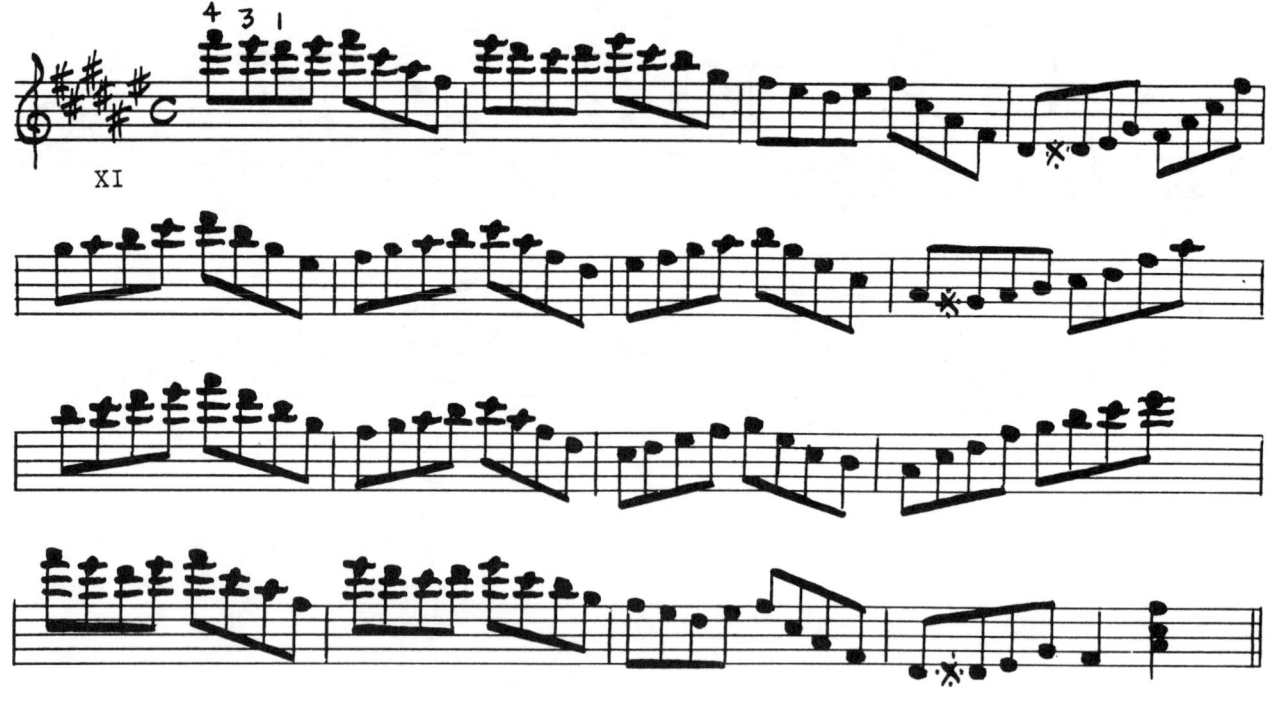
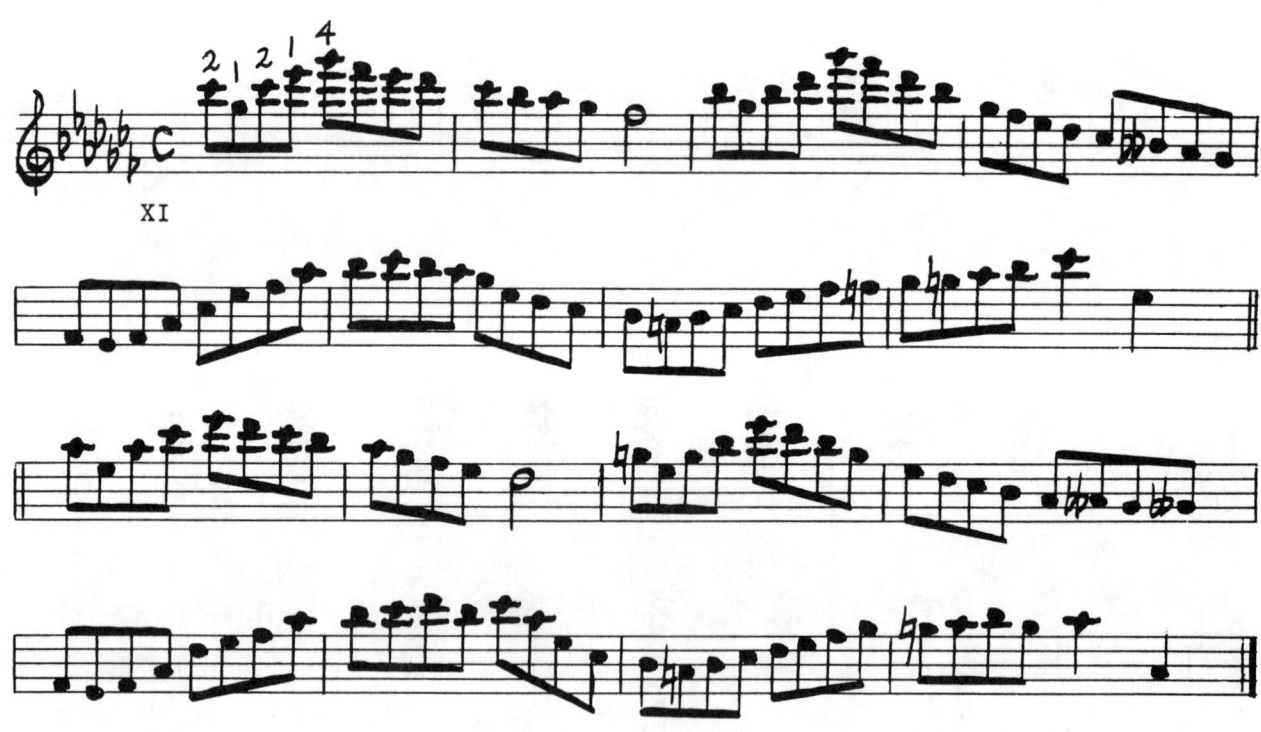

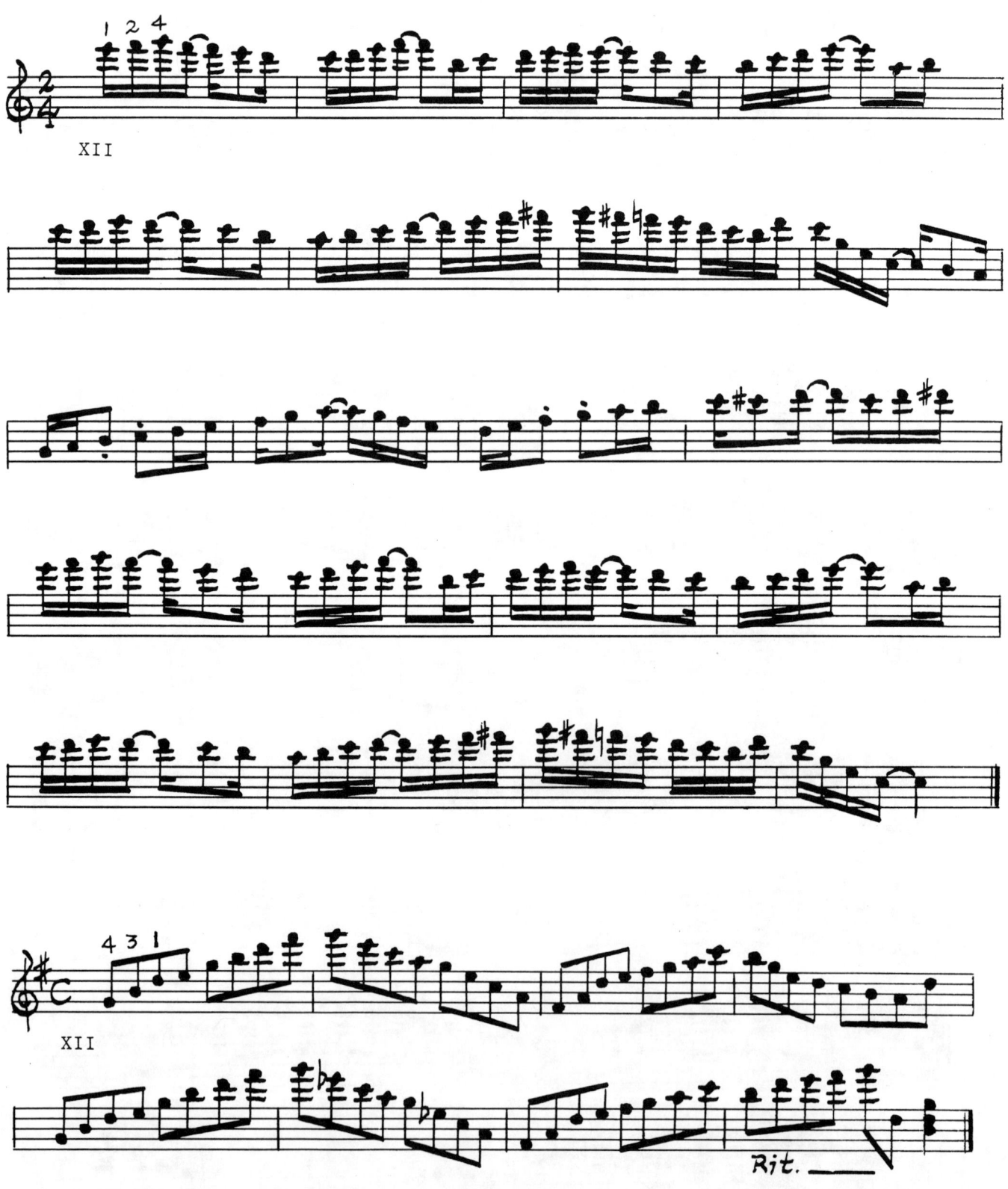

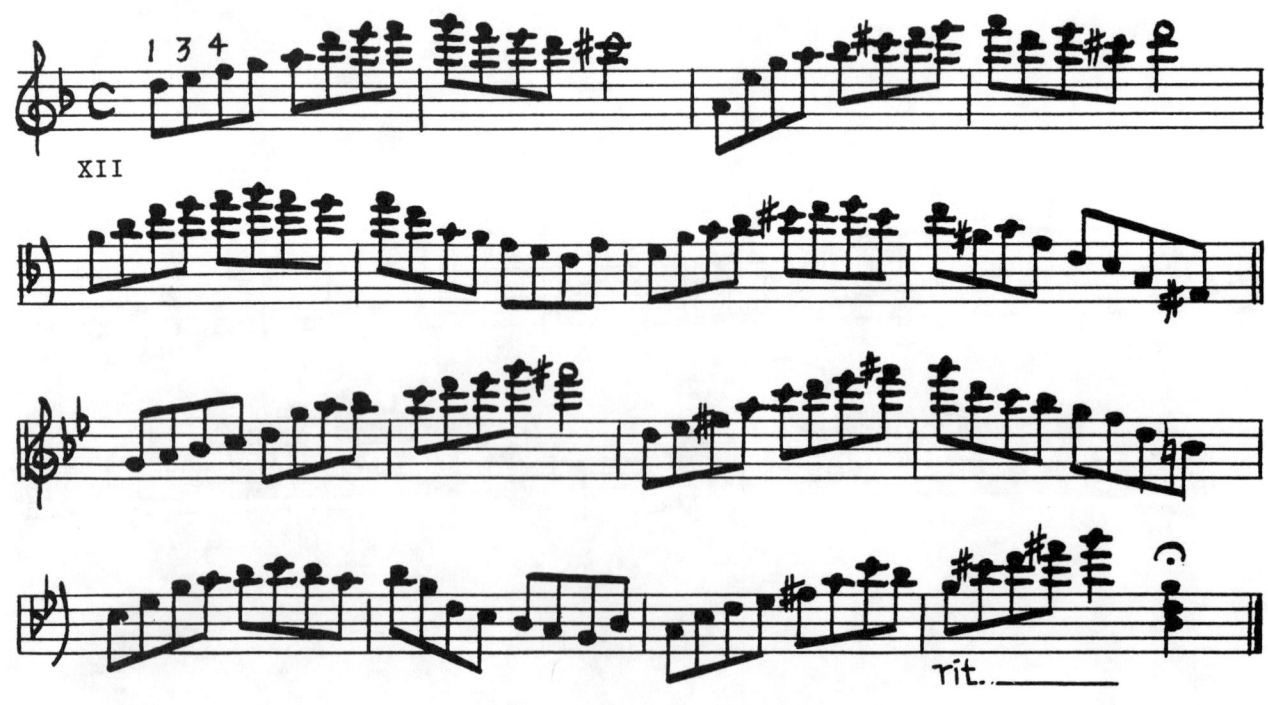

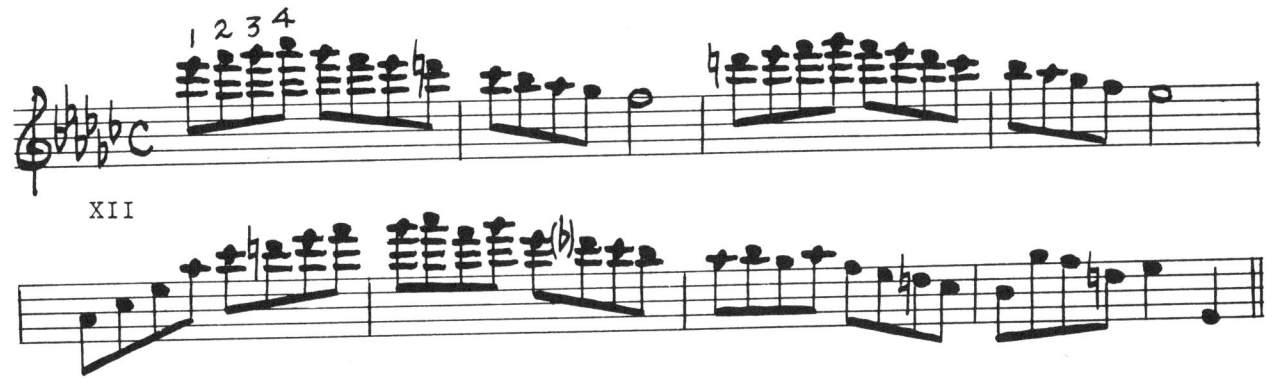

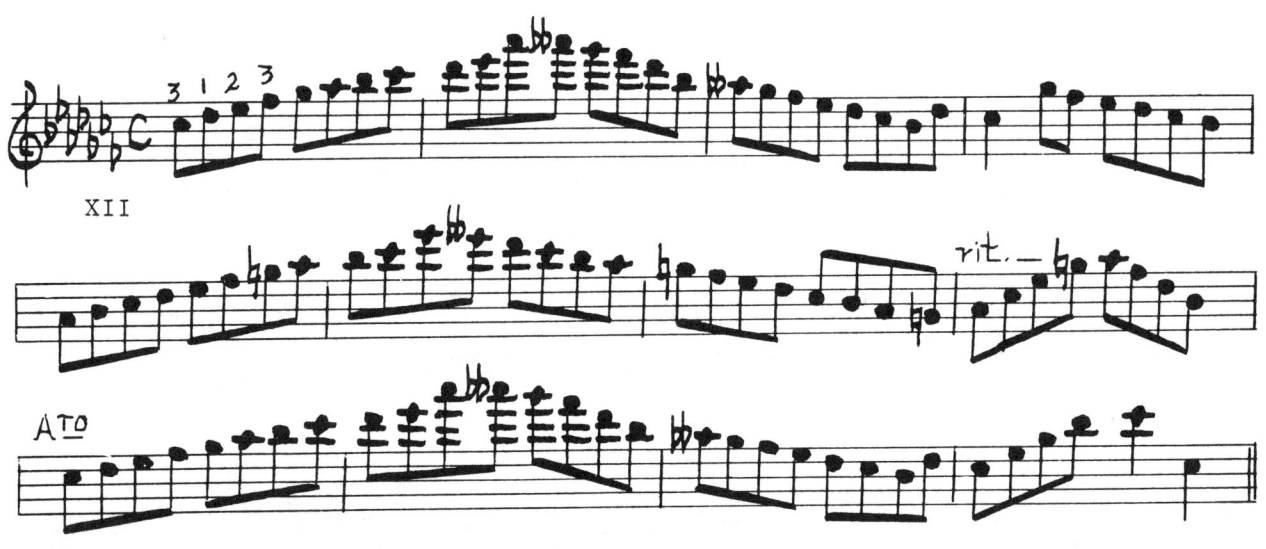

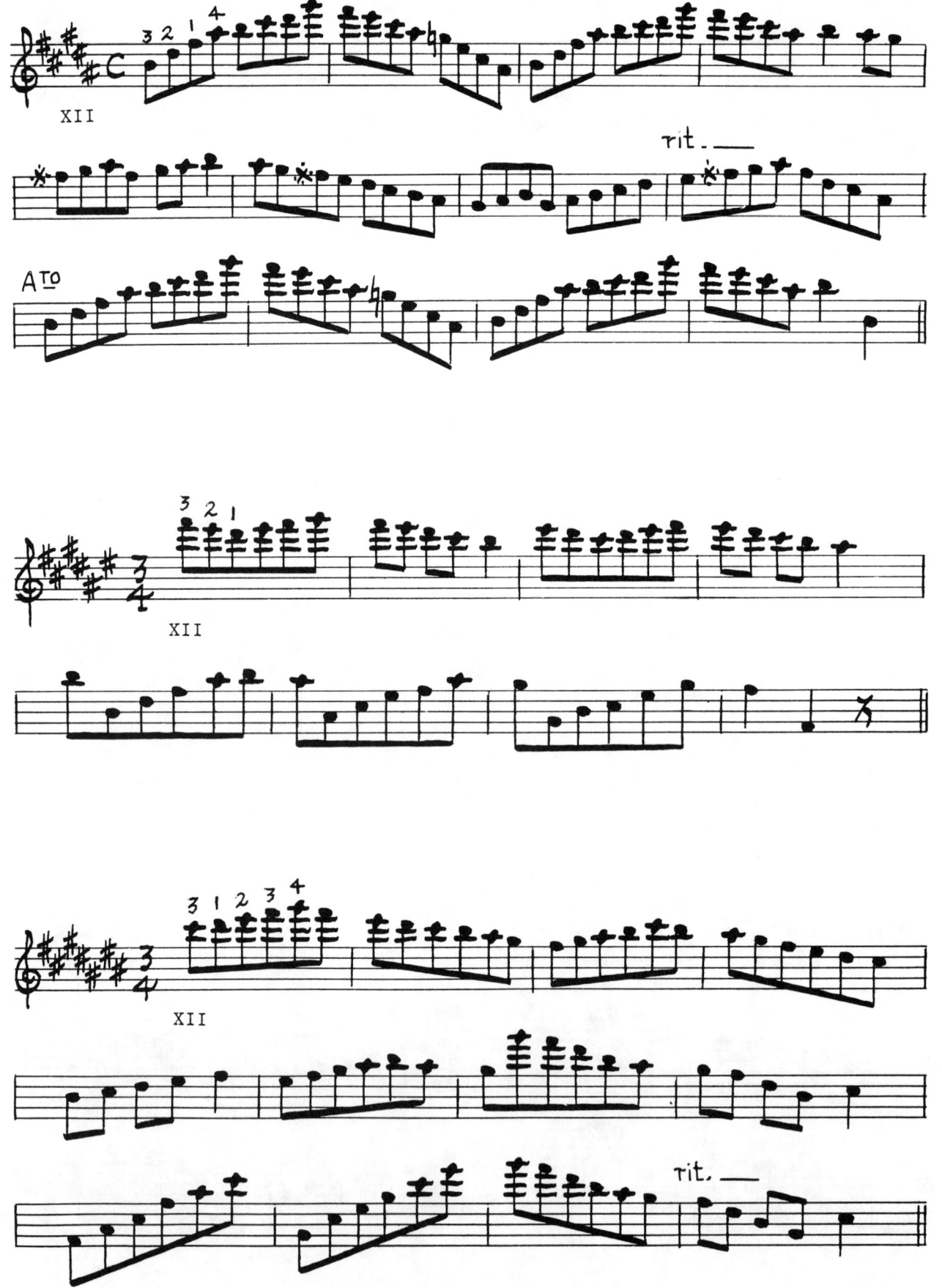

## MULTI-POSITION STUDIES

(These studies require more than one position for performance...
...you must work out the when and how for the pos. shifts.)

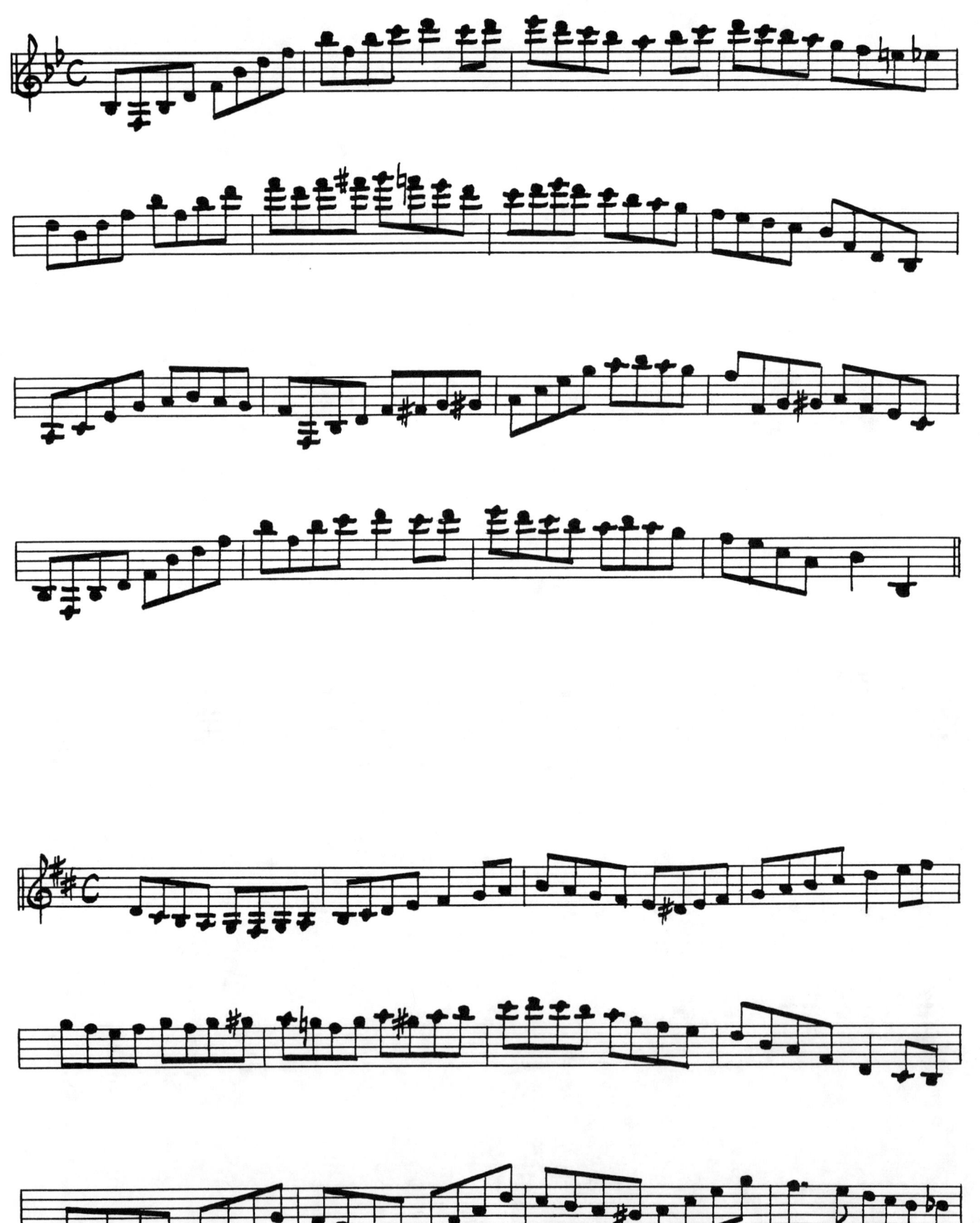

94

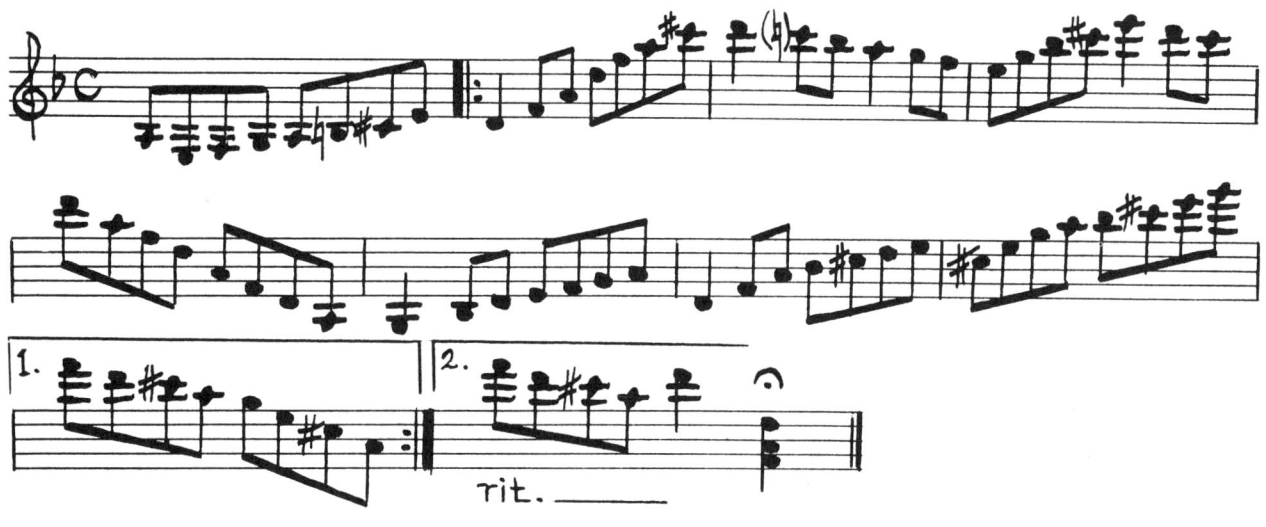
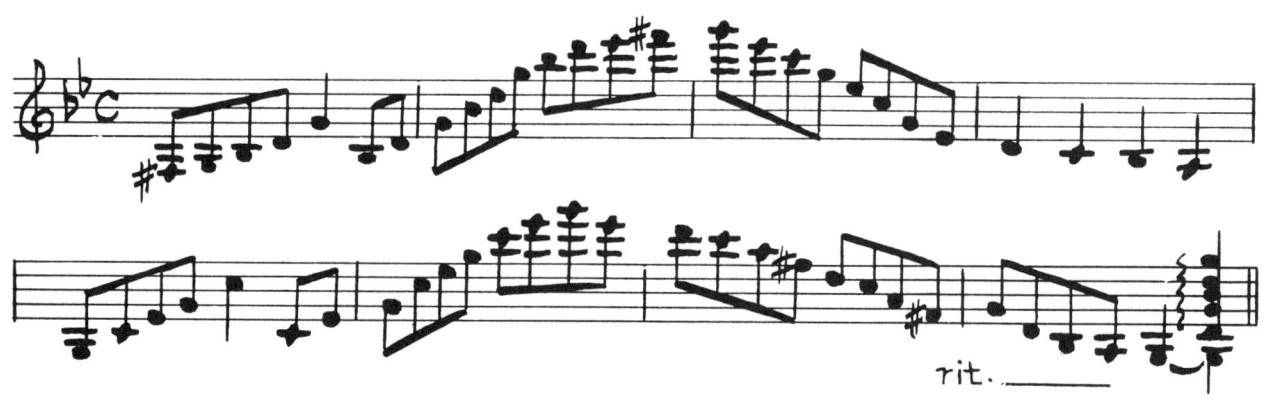

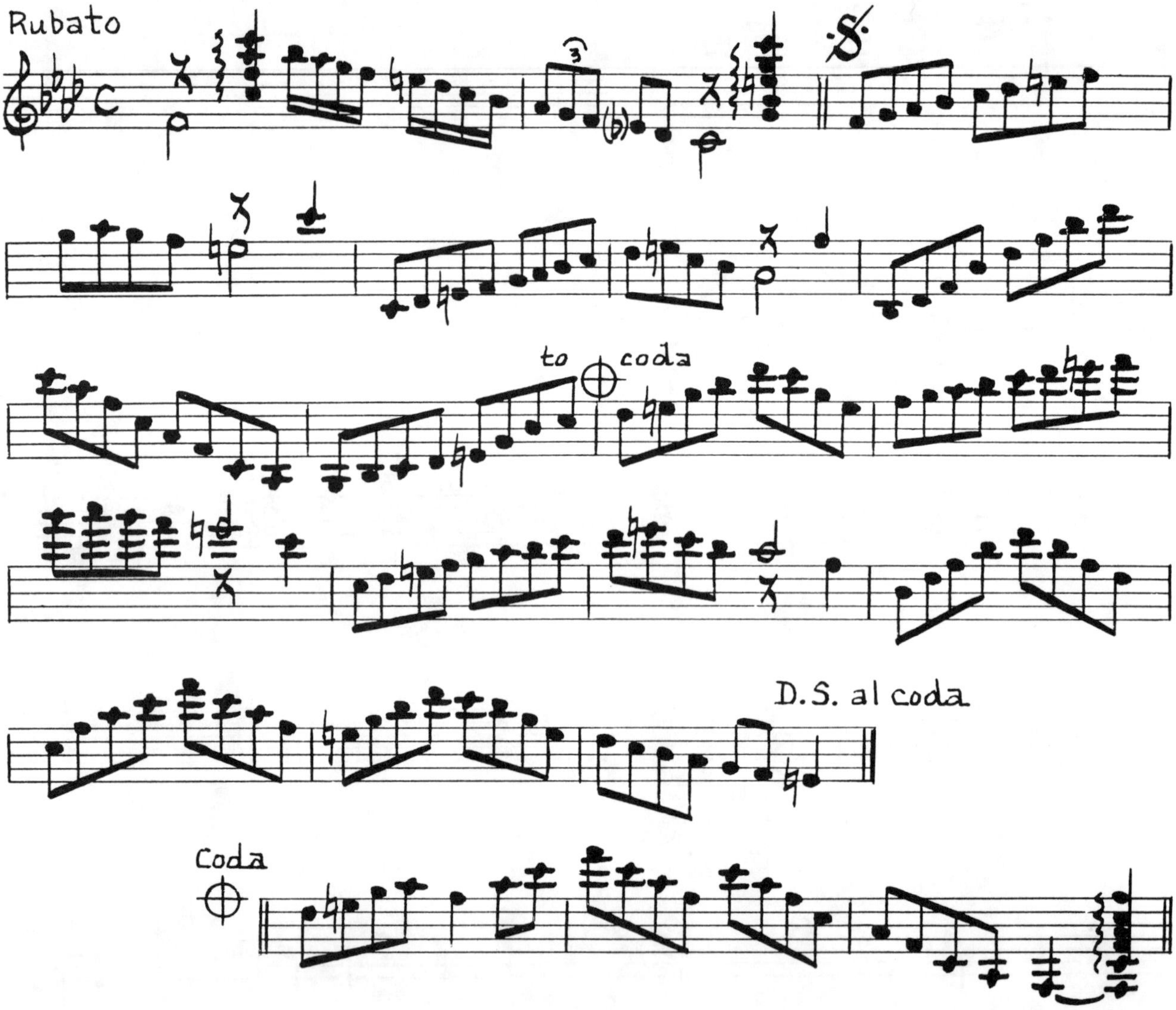
Rubato
3
(♭)
to coda
D.S. al coda
Coda

rit.

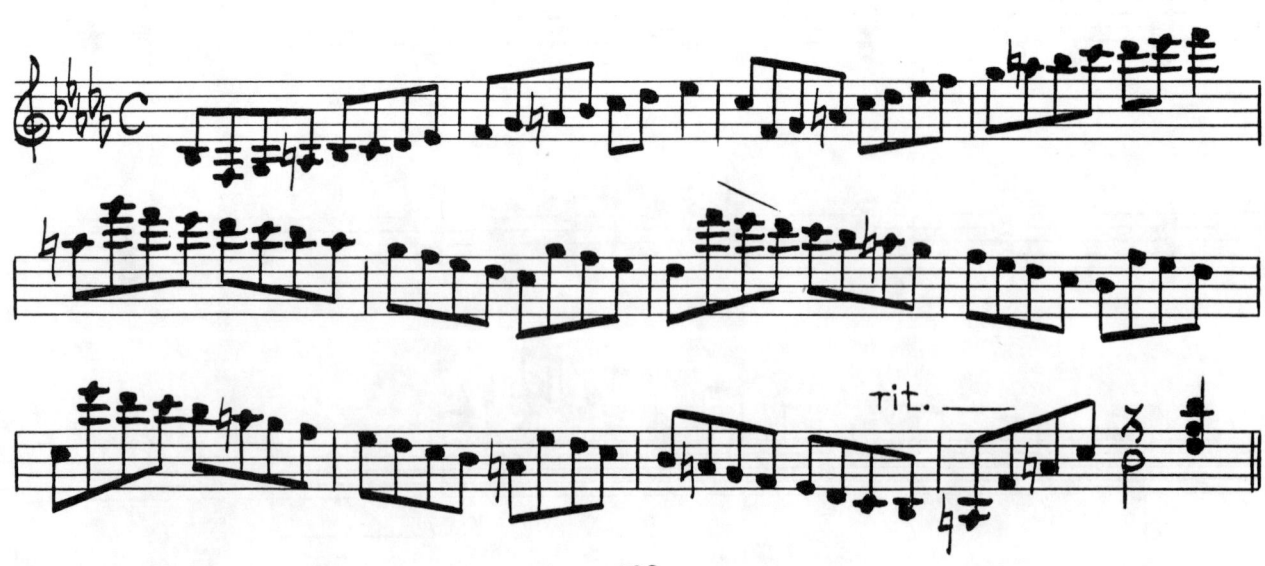

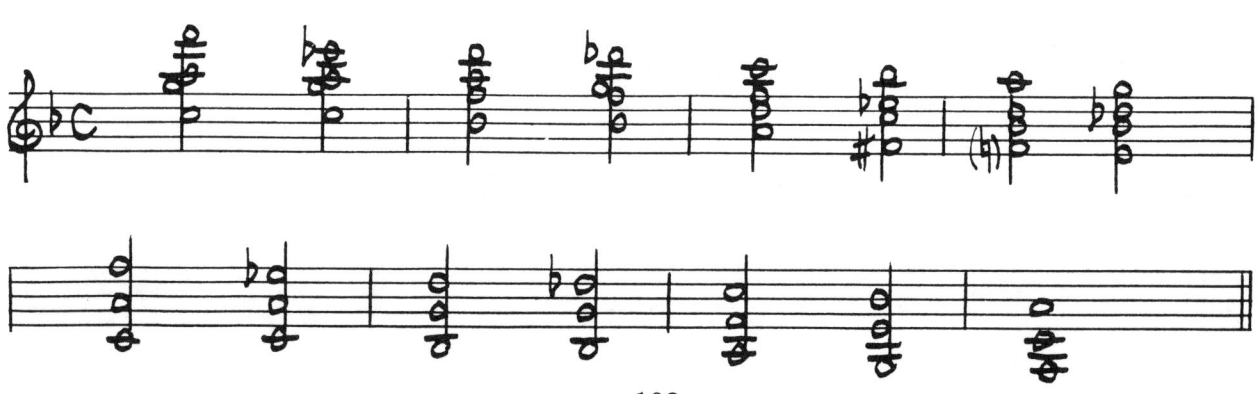

105

106

111